Praise for

Grief to Gratitude

"A compassionate guide through grief, this book blends profound spiritual insight with practical tools. Its journaling prompts and reframing of death from the loved one's perspective help shift pain into peace. A wise reminder to surrender, allow, and let life unfold through love."

GARRET YOUNT, PhD, Institute of Noetic Sciences, author of *Why Vibes Matter*

"Steven Ferrara has hit a home run! *Grief to Gratitude* speaks directly to the energizing core of each thinking soul. Based on his early exposure to Dr. Thurman Fleet's Concept-Therapy® teachings, Steven takes us on an evolutionary journey in becoming a more integrated, developed human soul. Read it and grow!"

CHARLES AND EMILY MATTOX, instructors at the Concept-Therapy Institute, San Antonio, Texas

"Through unimaginable loss, the author offers a profound reflection on grief, love, and the unexpected depths of learning that emerge from our darkest moments. It changed the way I see life—and learning—forever. Whether you've experienced deep loss or are simply navigating a hard season, this book will give you a new perspective on what it means to grow, to endure, and to truly live."

MARLO LYONS, career, executive, and team coach; award-winning author of *Wanted → A New Career*

"This book you hold is pure alchemy. Allow Steve's journey to transmute the idea of loss and grief into a truthful and honest understanding that death is merely a new beginning. You deserve to know that 'no loss' is a very real thing."

JOSEPH TEDESCO, TLC, speaker, coach, and consultant, Mindset Management

"This book is like having a wise, loving friend walk beside you, a light in the dark, a reminder that you are not alone—and that love and connection never end."

LUCI BUTLER WILLIAMS, author, composer, and sound healer, toured the world with the Trans-Siberian Orchestra as a keyboard player and vocalist

"*Grief to Gratitude* is an elegant contribution to humanity's current ascension. I found myself connecting with Steven's humanity, weeping and laughing with him as he shared the most intimate experiences of losing his beloved son, Christopher, and Steven's connecting to the essence of his son's soul through the ascension of his own humanity. Prepare to be guided through a multidimensional exploration of your own humanity through Steven's example, and witness the receiving of practical wisdom for which human beings have striven for millennia—gratitude, love, grace, and ultimately, joy."

RICARDO BROCKMANN, divine healer

"Steven Ferrara offers a rare perspective on grief and loss—one that reveals the beautiful truth that love and connection continue beyond the physical."

SAM WILLIAMS, world-touring musician and sound healer

Grief to Gratitude

Embracing *the* Inner Pathway *to* Healing *and* Peace

STEVEN A. FERRARA

www.amplifypublishinggroup.com

Grief to Gratitude: Embracing the Inner Pathway to Healing and Peace

For more information, please contact:
Amplify Publishing, an imprint of Amplify Publishing Group
620 Herndon Parkway, Suite 220
Herndon, VA 20170
info@amplifypublishing.com

Library of Congress Control Number: 2025912144

CPSIA Code: PRV0825A

ISBN-13: 979-8-89138-811-6

Printed in United States

To all those suffering through grief and life's deepest challenges—there is a pathway to healing and inner peace.

Contents

Foreword

FROM THE VERY FIRST pages of *Grief to Gratitude: Embracing the Inner Pathway to Healing and Peace*, Steve Ferrara draws you into a deeply personal and profoundly transformative journey after the loss of his twenty-three-year-old son, Christopher, in a car accident. This is no ordinary memoir about grief; it is a guide to understanding life, death, and the profound spiritual growth that can emerge from even the most painful experience.

What makes this book so extraordinary is Steve's openness and vulnerability. He shares his story with honesty and compassion, and his bringing us into his very personal journaling is what makes it so deeply moving. He doesn't shy away from the raw pain of loss or the struggles that come with it. Instead, he takes us by the hand and walks us through his journey, step by step, showing us how he moved from heartbreak to acceptance and from resistance to gratitude.

This is a book you won't want to put down; it is truly a page-turner. Steve's storytelling is so compelling that it kept me up late into the night, eager to keep reading and discover what came next. His ability to hold your attention and connect with you on such a deep level is a testament to his authenticity and the power of his message.

He doesn't offer quick solutions or easy answers. Instead, he shares his doubts, his questions, and his evolving insights, which ultimately amount to a road map of what is possible, showing us that even in our darkest moments, we can find acceptance, embrace the opportunity for growth, and ultimately discover profound gratitude.

If you are someone who is facing grief, struggling with understanding life's purpose, or seeking meaning amid tragedy, Steve assures us that no matter where we are in our own grieving process—no matter how insurmountable the challenge may seem—not only is there a pathway forward to healing, peace, and fulfillment, but that these outcomes are inevitable when we remain truly open.

This book is a testament to the resilience of the human spirit, a guiding light for anyone seeking to grow, and a gift that assures us that the transformation of grief to gratitude is indeed possible. In fact. Steve's insights into the nature of the universe and consciousness offer us not only a new way of understanding loss, but of understanding life itself.

As you turn the page and embark on sharing this journey with Steve, keep your heart and your mind open. If you do, this book may well change your life.

JACK CANFIELD, coauthor of *Chicken Soup for the Grieving Soul* and *The Success Principles™: How to Get from Where You Are to Where You Want to Be*

Preface

THE SUDDEN DEATH OF a loved one is a journey that no one expects or plans for. In my case, the death of my twenty-three-year-old son Christopher changed my life forever, ultimately guiding me to a state of heightened awareness and inner peace. This journey expanded my perspective and brought me to a new understanding of death and its meaning in life. I never intended to write a book about this experience, but over time, this book emerged from the hundreds of hours I spent journaling in the weeks, months, and years after Christopher's passing. These journals form a record of the emotional twists and turns I lived through, the questions I asked, and the many lessons I learned along the way.

Up until my son's death, I had been infrequent in my journaling, but I quickly realized that this practice was going to be a critical part of moving forward and healing from this unimaginable loss. I began to journal daily, primarily to open up a new type of communication with Christopher. I would start writing as if I were having a normal conversation with him, and that would often lead me to express the enormous grief I was going through, as well as the small steps I was taking toward healing. I didn't overthink these conversations, but entered them with an open mind and followed my stream of consciousness in the hope of finding guidance.

I had already begun to recognize that normal thinking had no answers for the intense emotions of grief. But as I allowed my stream of consciousness to flow, I stumbled across new levels of understanding. Slowly, this understanding deepened, leading me to the new perspective on death—and most of all, on life—that I'll be sharing in this book.

It has been many years since Christopher died, and I never looked back on my journals until writing this book. My journals still take me back to the raw and inconceivable grief of the early days, weeks, and months, and I can still cry intensely when I read them. I also see more clearly the bursts of understanding that emerged through the pain, and feel the indescribable love I discovered within—a love that has led me forward from a parent's most dreadful nightmare to find a grateful heart, which is the ultimate healing. Depending on where you are in your journey, that love and gratitude may feel far away or even unattainable, but I will do my best to show how I arrived at these insights, and assure you that there is peace and joy ahead.

I wrote this book to relieve the suffering of others by sharing what I've learned. Going back to read the journals and extract these lessons has turned out to be an exercise for my growth, for which I am so grateful. I humbly offer them in the hopes that they will help anyone who is going through a loss to become more aware of the love and peace that exist within, both during this life and beyond.

Chapter 1

Life Changes Completely

To my son Christopher,

As I write this, the morning after your death, I have so many questions and sometimes think I have answers, but they are not correct. All I know—all I hope—is that your physical death was without pain or fear and that you, your soul, and your consciousness are in a good or better place.

Mom and I are so fortunate to have been chosen to be your parents and the ones who gave you physical life. We love you physically, mentally, and spiritually. Although we don't have you any longer physically or mentally, we do and always will have you spiritually. Our job now is to learn how to enjoy this spiritual relationship with you. We will find our way back to happiness and joy and a fulfilling life with your guidance.

Love forever and eternity,
Dad

MY WIFE ALIE AND I were awakened suddenly at our home in Colt's Neck, New Jersey, when the local police knocked on our door. It was shortly after 6:00 a.m., and the sky was still dark. As we stood at the front door, the chilly December air blowing in, they told us that our son Christopher had been in a car accident and that we needed to go to the Jersey Shore Hospital Emergency Room immediately. We asked the officers if he was okay, and they were smart enough to tell us that they had no further information. Alie and I didn't know at the time that police would only come to someone's home if the worst had happened.

Christopher had just turned twenty-three the day before. He was our oldest child and a protective brother to his younger sisters: Dani, nineteen, and Alex, who had just turned eight. After attending college in Florida, he'd recently moved home to join the family business selling insurance and other financial products. He'd spent the day of his birthday in his sales manager's office, laying out a detailed plan for how to win the coveted National New Associate of the Year award in the coming year.

When he returned from the day's meetings, he relaxed on the couch with Dani for a while before going out to celebrate his birthday with friends at a popular live music bar nearby. "I love you! Remember to lock the door," he called to Dani as he walked out. Alie and I had already wished him a good night when we left earlier with our younger daughter Alex to see the neighborhood Christmas light decorations.

We figured Christopher would come home late, and we didn't wait up. Now, we were in a panic. Alie and I raced to get dressed. The commotion woke Dani up, and she came out of her room to ask us what was going on. When we told her that Chris was in the hospital, she insisted on coming with us.

Like all little sisters, Dani looked up to her big brother. They'd grown up together, played together, and spent countless hours building a closeness that only siblings can know and feel toward one another. As they were only four years apart, the two of them spent more time with each other than with anyone else in their lives. Now that they were both young adults, Dani and Chris had been finding even more in common and building the bond of their relationship even closer. Chris always made sure that his sister was safe, and all of their many friends were very close. Dani innately felt something that early Sunday morning and knew that she needed to be with us to see Christopher at the hospital.

We left Alex home with my in-laws, who lived in a house behind ours, promising to update them as soon as we had any information. The twenty-minute drive to the hospital was filled with dread, but we tried to keep ourselves calm by telling ourselves we could handle whatever condition Christopher was in. He was young and strong, an athlete; we felt he could make a complete recovery from just about anything. We pulled up to the emergency area, left our car at the front door, and ran inside. As we entered the hospital, we heard a young man's voice crying out in pain. I felt a strange wave of relief. If Chris was well enough to be making that sound, it meant he was going to be okay.

A nurse ushered us into a room and told us to wait. It felt like hours but was only minutes before the head nurse entered the room with a serious look on her face. We asked her how Chris was doing, fully expecting to be told about injuries that, no matter how dire, we knew he would overcome thanks to his perfect health, build, attitude, and strength. With a mix of compassion and sympathy, the nurse told us that Chris had been brought to the hospital at about 2:00 a.m. and was dead on arrival. As I write this, I still can't believe I am saying this all these years later.

Alie, Dani, and I grabbed each other and cried hysterically in a tight hug for a very long time. It is impossible for the mind to process this unimaginable reality. There is no thinking, which would not be any help anyway, just pure, primal, raw emotion of a type unlike any I have ever felt and hope to never feel again. It takes control of your body to the point of uncontrollable shaking; visceral, uncontainable crying; and an exhausting struggle to breathe. The nurse stoically stayed in the room as we struggled to comprehend this incomprehensible shock. It felt like we would stay there, crying, forever. But after a long time, Alie raised her head and spoke to the nurse. "I want to see my son," she said.

Farewell to Our Beautiful Son

When Alie said she wanted to see Chris, I wasn't sure I could handle it. I had no idea what to expect but anticipated the worst. I feared that his body may have been horribly injured, disfigured, or even mangled, leaving us with images we could never unsee. But I trusted Alie. She was the cornerstone of our family, a loving wife and mother whose absolute priority in life was raising our children and creating a warm and welcoming home. With her traditional German upbringing, she was also the family disciplinarian, upholding a sense of order, responsibility, and routine. Alie and I had gotten married when we were barely out of our teens and had finished growing up together, never wavering from our commitment to each other and our children.

The three of us followed the nurse into a small, sterile, brightly lit room. We were all still shaking uncontrollably from the shock, fear, and disbelief that grips you in such moments. There was Chris, lying under a blanket with his head uncovered. He looked like the same beautiful, handsome Christopher he'd always been, his black hair thick and shiny, his expression calm, with not one scratch other than a small mark on the tip of his chin. His body was unharmed, and as we soon found out, his cause of death was drowning in the lake that his car went into. He showed no signs of trauma or suffering.

We hugged and kissed his cold body, caressed his hair, and cried together for a long time. Alie cried with a primal rawness that only a mother can feel, her thin body shaking; Dani clung to her older brother, her face drenched in tears. We didn't want to leave the room. It felt like leaving would mean accepting Chris's death and making it real and permanent, and how could we bear to do that? But eventually, the nurse approached us, and in a very caring and compassionate way, she escorted us out of the room.

Alie, Dani, and I were physically, mentally, and emotionally exhausted from crying, but we reluctantly walked out into the hallway. The nurse asked if we needed someone to drive us home or if we wanted to make a phone call. I said that I was okay to drive but told her I wanted to call my father first so that someone other than us knew what had happened. I also knew that someone had to start telling the rest of our family the utterly unthinkable and incomprehensible.

My father Al was my best friend other than Chris. He was a kind and loving man, a musician, a businessman, and a spiritual seeker. When I was eight years old, his good friend introduced him to the Concept Therapy Institute founded by Dr. Thurman Fleet in San Antonio, Texas. This comprehensive course of spiritual studies put him on his lifelong journey and became the foundation for my interest in the deeper meanings of life. At the age of eighteen, I'd joined him in the insurance business. Since then, we'd spent countless hours together, carpooling to the office, grabbing lunch at diners, and even teaching spiritual and personal development classes together on the weekends. We'd lived two blocks apart for many years and got to spend an inordinate amount of time with each other, enjoying every aspect of our relationship.

Now, I fished my cell phone out of my pocket and called my dad's number. He answered in his usual cheerful manner. But when I heard his voice, I was overcome by one of the strongest waves of emotion I had ever felt in my life. It seemed that the muscles of my face were in spasm, and I couldn't speak or even make a sound. Never before had I felt so helpless, unable to utter a word—the basic physical and mental faculties on which I depended not responding, leaving only this terrible pain.

The nurse gently took the phone and told my father the unimaginable. I can't even begin to guess what my amazing, wise, spiritual, eighty-year-old father felt at that moment. Christopher was his first grandson, and they had a bond based in love, respect, and mutual interests in business, philosophy, and spirituality. Since Chris had become the third generation to join the family business, this bond had grown even deeper. I wished I could somehow protect him from the heart-wrenching shock and pain.

Alie, Dani, and I drove home in total silence. When we walked into the house, which was a large home we had built only a few years ago that had huge rooms for entertaining with high, spacious ceilings, we went straight to our daughter Alex's room. We knew we had to be honest with her but weren't sure what to say. What can you say to a gentle and innocent little girl enjoying her wonderful little life? Due to the age difference of eleven and fifteen years with her older sister and brother, Alex had always been the baby. Dani and Christopher loved her and cared for her and, in many ways, got to experience what it would be like when they had their own children. Alex had brought a sense of peace and joy to our family ever since she'd been born. How could we shatter her world with this unimaginable loss of her brother.

We tried to keep it together as we told Alex that Chris would not be coming home. It seemed to make sense to tell her that he was now with God in Heaven because God needed him. I'm not sure that this made sense to her or even to us, but it seemed like the only thing to say. Her little mind could only take in the intense sadness that had overtaken our otherwise very happy home. We all cried for a long time, all of us in shock and unable to process the reality and permanence of the fact that we would never see Christopher again. The permanence of death is, by far, the hardest part to comprehend. But even though his physical form would no longer be with us, I already knew that our relationship with Christopher had to continue in some way.

Shockwaves of Grief

Shortly after we got home, our house began flooding with family and friends who were supposed to be coming that day for a double birthday party for Christopher and Alex, but were instead arriving in a state of disbelief, to provide us with support. Our long driveway filled up with cars, and it seemed that the news had traveled quickly through our community. There was hugging, crying, more hugging, and more crying as each new group of visitors arrived. Through my exhaustion, I was dimly aware of feeling grateful to have so many people around, as if they could somehow help carry the weight of this astonishing new reality. I remember my cousin, who is a policeman and must deal with tragic situations often, telling me to make sure I ate and got some sleep, neither of which was of interest to me.

That night, I fell asleep out of sheer exhaustion, then woke before dawn. After the temporary relief of unconsciousness, it was torture to wake up and remember all over again that Christopher was gone. I tiptoed out of our bedroom, not wanting to wake Alie. I slowly made my way to the kitchen, pulled out a spiral-bound notebook with a hard black cover, and sat down at the table to journal.

As my pen scratched the paper, I felt a strong sense of Christopher's presence—as if he hadn't died at all but had only stepped out for a minute. Maybe this was where I would meet with Chris now: on the pages of this journal, where I could speak with him in the privacy of my own heart. It wasn't the same as hugging him close, but it was real, alive, and more urgent than ever.

When the sun rose, a fresh flood of people began to arrive, as would continue to happen for many days and even weeks. The pain and grief were physically and mentally crippling, and there was no relief. Everyone naturally did their best to be strong for us, but they were also going through their own grief, because Chris had meaningful relationships with everyone in his life. Indeed, as more and more people heard the news, the shockwaves of grief spread outward, until it seemed that everyone we knew was grieving with us.

Chris was a physically and mentally strong person who had deep and significant love-based relationships with all of his family and friends. When he was only four years old, his preschool teacher had told Alie and me how Chris would run over to any child who was hurt or crying and console them. "You have a very special child," she said. A rough and tough preschooler who loved trucks, dinosaurs, and all the usual "boy things," Chris could nevertheless be sweet and tender, and his relationships came from the heart, even at a young age.

After just a few months in the family business, my colleagues were already commenting on Christopher's cheerful attitude, diligent work ethic, and willingness to help in any way. Along with his best friend Justin, who was also new to the firm, he'd get up bright and early and head to Dunkin' Donuts to greet all the local business owners getting their coffee. Justin and Christopher never tired of chatting with anyone and everyone who walked in the door, building relationships and reintroducing themselves to the community as young professionals.

Other new associates were inspired by the seemingly effortless way Christopher connected with people, paying close attention to their needs so he could put himself in service to them. Senior associates, most of whom had known Chris since he was a child, were eager to take him under their wing, as his fearlessness, enthusiasm, and love for our profession reawakened a sense of excitement in them.

A colleague of mine who had lost his son to a rare case of malaria only fourteen weeks before Chris's death was one of the many who came to visit us in those first few days. He was still deep in his own pain, and I remember thinking that making it another fourteen minutes seemed impossible, let alone fourteen weeks. I wondered how he'd made it that far. If grief was a normal part of being human, we must be designed to handle it. So why did it feel like it was breaking me apart?

Seeing Chris Through Many Eyes

Alie and I forced ourselves to do what needed to be done after Chris's death, including the traditional funeral services. Well over one thousand people attended the four-hour service. Relatives and friends filled the funeral home and lined up outside in the bitter cold for hours. Traffic was blocked around all of the streets due to the enormous outpouring of love for Chris that day. We kept the service very simple, with only my father, sister, and a good friend of the family saying a few words about Chris. Nothing really needed to be said, because everyone had their own relationship with him and already knew how amazing he was.

After the funeral, Alie and I invited everyone back to our home, and hundreds of people came. Everyone did whatever needed to be done: ordering, cooking, and serving food and drink; cleaning up; and answering the door and phone, all while being so attentive and supportive to Alie and me and our girls and anything we may have needed. Somehow, everything got handled perfectly, and this continued for many days and weeks.

His friends put together four collages with hundreds of pictures of Chris's life, showing him beaming in his high school graduation gown, being playful and funny with family and friends, flexing his muscles at the gym, and dressed up for prom with his girlfriend. There were even pictures from Thanksgiving with family just a few weeks before. I have these collages framed in our home and look at them often for inspiration as well as for the strong feeling of love they still emanate.

Christmas was only a week after Chris died—a torturous time for our entire family. We quickly realized we were not in a mindset for anything festive, but found solace in sharing stories about Chris: how he would put on a leather jacket and sing along to the movie *Grease* when he was seven years old, pretending he was Danny Zuko; the time he and his friends got in trouble for throwing a lawnmower in a pool; and how he used to tell me I was so good at basketball I could be in the NBA—until he got old enough to realize that maybe I'd be better off merely *coaching* in the NBA. Finally, as he began to beat me more and more often during our games on the driveway basketball court, he concluded that I might be better off simply being a *fan* of the NBA.

Chris had already done his Christmas shopping, and we decided to look through the many shopping bags he had in his room. We found four boxes of Happy Feet slippers: one pair each for Alie, Dani, Alex, and me. Each pair was shaped like a different animal, and they came with a story about how these slippers keep you happy when you wear them. This felt like the first of many messages we would receive from Christopher, and wow, did we need it. We wore those slippers 24/7 and later ordered another two hundred pairs to give to our family and friends in memory of Chris's happy and enthusiastic attitude toward life.

Chris's many friends would stop by frequently in those early days and weeks and tell us stories about him. His beautiful high school girlfriend would tell us that Chris was the most loving, caring, and attentive boyfriend that any girl could ask for. Other friends shared stories of Christopher's excellence and skill at soccer, his passion for the gym, and the ways he'd inspired them to work toward their goals. With each story, I felt that I was seeing Chris through new eyes—and every set of eyes showed me another side to my beautiful son, whom I thought I had known so well. He was deeply beloved by many different people, for many different reasons, and in many different ways.

His girlfriend, Tieal, whom Chris planned to marry, was devastated by Chris's death. A tall, athletic, blonde woman who'd attended the same university as Chris on a full soccer scholarship, Tieal was everything our family could ask for in a future daughter-in-law and mother to our grandchildren. She told me that during their two-year relationship, Chris taught her how to open her heart, be vulnerable, and love someone. Although they'd started off as friends, Chris and Tieal's relationship quickly grew serious, and during the many runs they took together around the college campus, they used to imagine their shared future—a future that would never happen now.

Over the course of these conversations with Tieal and Christopher's friends and our family, I learned so many things about Chris that I hadn't known: that he wanted to build a family and a life just like Alie and I had built, because he loved his upbringing and respected the fact that family was everything to us. That he would decide to leave a party before his friends and walk home on his own, sometimes for miles, through freezing or inclement weather, just because he preferred to be home with our family. That he bought Tieal twenty-one birthday cards on her twenty-first birthday and dreamed of buying her a car as soon as his career got going.

That his favorite Maroon 5 song was "She Will Be Loved," and he would sing it at the top of his lungs to Tieal when they were driving together. That his passion for every aspect of life was inspiring and that he provided advice and wisdom beyond his years to so many. That Dani felt a sense of calm and safety when she came home and Chris was in his bedroom next to hers. That he was always interested in whatever she had done that day. That Alex loved when Chris picked her up and threw her around, and how she would laugh so hard when he chased our dog Charlie around the house.

There were hundreds of stories that helped me see the breadth and depth of Chris beyond the amazing version of him that I knew in our father-son relationship. He had so many sides to him that I didn't know, reflecting different pieces of himself and building unique relationships with everyone he met. I could never hear enough of these stories and clung to each one, as I felt they continued to broaden my loving relationship with him. I began to realize that, as much as I knew about him as his father, it was only one small slice of his life and experiences. Christopher's journey was about so much more than the relationship he shared with me. Was there a way I could continue to support his journey?

Hitting Rock Bottom

It felt comforting to have so many people around, all of them carrying a piece of Chris. But I also needed to do a lot of processing on my own. In addition to sadness, I was boiling with extreme anger beyond anything I had ever felt. The only thing I could do to express this anger was to take a run through the open countryside where we lived and scream at the top of my lungs. I would run for miles down the long country roads during the freezing winter months that followed Chris's death, yelling at God for what He had done, or at least allowed to happen, tears running down my face.

I felt so angry, so confused, so lost. How could this fun-loving, caring, compassionate, hardworking, enthusiastic, wonderful, and loving son of ours have his bright future taken away? How could God put my daughters through the experience of losing their big brother and Tieal through the experience of losing her fiancé? This had to be a mistake.

I remember one day shortly after Chris's passing when my father was at my house. I was so sad, missing Chris and crying, my knees weak and my whole body racked with pain. He cradled my face in both hands as only a loving father can do, his expression so gentle. I looked into his eyes, my body bent over as if I'd been punched in the stomach, and said, "Dad, it hurts so bad."

At that moment, my father and I looked deeply into each other's souls. He was the man who had always given me so many answers, and he could only look back at me with his own grief. In his infinite wisdom, he just experienced this moment with me, and we shared it in powerful silence. We then hugged and cried for a while, and that was about as good an answer as I could ever ask from the man who was always there for me.

Looking back, I see that moment with my father as hitting rock bottom. Standing in our kitchen, I realized there was no answer that I would ever get from the outside, and that my thought-based mind had nothing to offer but a loop of intense loss, sadness, and grief. My mind had always served me well: making plans, serving up clever solutions to problems, and analyzing situations. But now, it felt like my mind had become useless: only providing looping thoughts of what-ifs and what-could-have-beens. I would dwell on the injustice of losing Chris, comb through all the things I "could have done differently" to stop him from dying that night, and imagine all the life experiences he would never have.

The thought-based tools of projecting into the future or dwelling on the past keep our minds busy, but they cannot give us answers to life's biggest questions, and they cannot lead us to peace. If my mind couldn't help me make sense of Christopher's death, what hope was there? I felt desperate, raw, and ready to collapse. But contained within this rock-bottom moment was a small opening that felt like hope. Somewhere *beyond* thought, I knew there had to be other tools for dealing with this unimaginable experience. I was not yet ready to see more than a tiny glimmer of this truth at the time. But a single thought floated into my mind: *There has to be a better way.*

This desperate cry came from the deepest part of my being. It cracked open a door that went far beyond the thought-based portion of my mind and eventually led me to discover the calm and peaceful essence beyond thought.

I knew in that moment that something inside me had shifted, but I did not yet realize how powerful that shift was going to be.

Chapter 2

The Process of Grieving

Hi Chris,

I love you so very, very much. I still cannot fully believe that I will not see you again during this life.

I realize that I do not understand much about life and death, about the purpose of many things that happen, and certainly why you were taken and/or at some level chose to leave your human life. I have many thoughts and theories, but nothing that I feel I really know.

Help me understand where you are and how you are doing.

Help me understand life and death and the purpose of both.

Help me know you are close to me. I want to feel you and know you are near.

Help me fully understand in order to move on in my human life with purpose and happiness and love for all.

Love forever and eternity,
Dad

THE HOLIDAYS HAD NOW passed. During those early weeks, I only wanted to be with my wife and daughters or other close family with whom I could talk about Chris. I wanted to wrap myself in the stories and memories that made me feel connected to him and that kept him alive and present in my mind. At the same time, I knew I couldn't spend the rest of my life in my sweatpants, crying and reminiscing, doing the bare minimum of taking care of myself. I had my wife and two beautiful daughters to live for. I knew that moving forward was the only option—but how?

Shortly after New Year's, I tried to get back to my routines at work. I'd always enjoyed running my business. It gave me a sense of structure, purpose, and drive. I loved buttoning up my suit, slicking back my hair, and being on my A game every day. Even though I was more introverted than most people realized, I nevertheless enjoyed walking through the office, greeting everyone like family and doing whatever I could to help them thrive in their positions. Maybe going back to the office would prop me up and keep me from sliding into the pool of self-pity whose constant beckoning I was so determined to resist.

However, going back to work wasn't as straightforward as I'd hoped. I showed up for meetings but was often in a daze and not always "there." My ability to focus had been profoundly affected by grief, and although I went through the motions, I found it difficult to embody the role that had once come so easily to me. Luckily, everyone in the firm was stepping up and supporting the daily management.

I remember a Monday meeting after a long weekend. As I walked out of the meeting, one of my managing partners, who had known Chris well and loved him, followed me into my office.

"Steven," he said. "The firm's in good shape, everyone is staying focused, and I'll be sure to handle all the phone calls coming in about Christopher."

He then gently informed me that my face was only shaved on one side, my suit was rumpled, and I looked exhausted.

"If you need more time at home, please take it," he said. "I'm here for you every step of the way."

My eyes misted with tears as I felt the immense kindness and sincerity of his words. It seemed to me I was receiving a gentle teaching. Maybe there was more to moving forward than putting on my suit and tie. Maybe the pain *was* the path—and the first step I had to take was to feel it deeply, without fear.

Emotions Must Be Embraced

After that conversation with my managing partner, I began to realize that the grieving process must be allowed. Each step is essential. Indeed, one cannot move forward *without* grieving. The painful emotions need to be expressed and even embraced; we need to let them in and experience them fully. All too often, however, our instinctual reaction is to bury them, push them aside, or ignore them, simply because they hurt so badly. We fear the pain will destroy us—but while it can be agonizing, the fact remains that it needs to be fully experienced in order to be released.

Even worse than pushing our painful emotions aside is when we dwell in them and allow them to control our lives. Instead of simply *feeling* our painful emotions, we spin stories of "what I could have done differently" or "what he will miss out on or could have been." The thought-based mind provides endless fuel for these stories, and no matter how many times we get hooked by them, it can be hard to accept that they always lead to dead ends. Instead of resolving our emotions, we end up bathing in sympathy and self-pity, endlessly reviewing all the scenarios that never happened, and never will.

The common approach to consoling a bereaved person can make this pattern even harder to break. When a loved one dies, well-meaning friends and relatives naturally want to express their sympathy. This deluge of sympathy can have the unintended effect of making it even more tempting to curl up in a ball, dwelling in the pain, and even clinging to it. When someone says, "I feel so bad for you," while it is meant to comfort, it can trigger self-pity or even a sense of victimhood—and those are the last things you need if you're going to move forward in a healthy way.

More often than not, it felt burdensome to see someone for the first time after Chris's death. We always had to go through the heavy interaction of trying to find words, and I began to feel that this painful ritual was more for their sake than mine. Sometimes, it felt like people left their grief on my shoulders, and I would literally have to shake it off.

I quickly realized that most of us are ill-equipped for dealing with death and can unwittingly do more harm than good when comforting a grieving friend. The traditional ways of acknowledging the death of a loved one can often create a heaviness for both the giver and receiver of condolences. Everyone is doing their best to say something they feel is helpful while trying to wrap their heads around the enormity of the experience; the results can be awkward for all parties involved. After so many of these heavy encounters, I found myself wondering, if words are no match for this unimaginable loss, could there be another way to express these intense feelings?

The Power of Silence

One day while Alie and I were out for a walk, we stopped by a little hotel where Chris used to work, doing every job from bellboy to pool boy to butler. He'd always spoken so highly of the owners, and we decided to go inside to see them. When we shared the sad message, they simply stood in silence, their eyes shining back all the love they had for Chris and all the sadness they felt. It was a surprising response, but a pleasant one. When nothing was verbalized, we could enjoy the quiet humanness and strong feeling of love that we shared with each other in that moment. We all knew that it emanated from the love we shared for Chris.

The hotel owners weren't the only ones to respond with silence. Several other friends and acquaintances did the same, responding with a hug or a gaze that communicated so much more than words ever could. In those moments, I felt witnessed and supported in my grief rather than burdened by well-meaning people. Instead of unknowingly piling their emotional pain on my shoulders, these quieter interactions had a feeling of acknowledgment at a deeper level. I could walk away from them with a feeling of lightness rather than an additional strain.

I was also discovering the power of silence in other aspects of my grieving process. Silence was a space in which I could feel Christopher's presence strongly, especially when I sat down with my journal. Sitting alone in a quiet place, with more calmness and clarity, I could reach out and touch him with my mind—indeed, with my very soul. Listening deeply, I could feel his presence within the silence, where I'd once found it in the familiar sound of his voice.

These quiet times were a powerful counterpart to the many hours of sharing Christopher stories with family and friends. He was there in the stories *and* in the silence; in the waves of emotion that came and went; and in the subtle flickers of insight that began to make themselves known, the more I learned to recognize them.

Going with Our Guts

One day toward the end of winter, my wife and I were having one of those very sad moments, hugging in the kitchen just before I left for the office. Just a few days before, our whole family had gone to my company's annual awards banquet, an extremely emotional event at which I gave a speech about Christopher and gifted the Happy Feet slippers we'd ordered to all the colleagues and associates who'd known Christopher so well. We'd shown a short video of his life, at the end of which everyone shared in the deep sadness while celebrating the person he was. Then, my partner invited Dani and Tieal up to the stage to receive two awards on Christopher's behalf. With tears running down their faces, he placed the plaques engraved with Christopher's name in their hands.

While the awards banquet was deeply meaningful, it was emotionally exhausting for all of us. In the days that followed, we all felt drained. Now, out of nowhere, Alie looked at me and said, "We need to move to Delray Beach."

Delray Beach is a lively seaside town in Florida, an hour north of Miami. We'd bought a condo there several years before, and ever since, it had become a place we associated with peace, joy, and relaxation. The university Chris and Tieal had attended, and from which Tieal would be graduating that spring, was only fifteen minutes down the road. We'd all loved the palm trees, the long sandy beaches, and the iguanas sunning themselves amid bright tropical flowers, but it had never occurred to us to move there full-time.

Now, without any hesitation or resistance, Alie and I saw in each other's eyes that this was a "eureka" moment. Together, we felt a knowingness that this was the right and only thing to do. With that strong conviction and a feeling of a higher purpose, we didn't think about what our family, my colleagues, or anyone else would say. In fact, we didn't think at all. We knew that we needed to make this change regardless of whether it aligned with "expert" advice on grieving or even made sense for us at a practical level. Instead, we went with our guts.

The following weekend, we headed to Florida with our daughters, on a mission to find a home. We soon found one that looked perfect for us, only to discover it wasn't for sale. Feeling slightly disheartened, we flew back to New Jersey. Was this a sign that our intuition had been wrong? Were we meant to stay in New Jersey, close to my office and to the many relatives and friends with whom Christopher had grown up? Was a move to Florida just too impractical?

But several days later, when Alie went through the new listings, she saw that the house we'd fallen in love with had come on the market. We immediately called our real estate agent.

"Well, the house already has an offer," he said. "But if you can get down here within twenty-four hours, there's still time to submit a higher one." This was long before electronic signatures and doing business remotely.

We booked a flight for the next morning, even though it was still winter in the Northeast and a snowstorm was predicted. Somehow, our flight was the last one to depart before the airport closed due to the storm. When we got to Delray Beach, we made an offer—and the sellers accepted.

The house in Delray Beach was even more perfect than we'd realized. It turned out that the original builders were the very same people who owned the small hotel where Chris had worked and who loved him so much. When we told Tieal the address, she gasped. "That's in the neighborhood where me and Chris used to go running," she said. "He always said he wanted to live there someday."

Was this a coincidence? An intervention from Chris? Who knows?

What I do know is that my family's healing process began to move forward in a big way after we took this step, and that Chris played a central role.

Moving to Delray Beach was a huge undertaking for which I give my wife all the credit. Over the next few months, she packed up the entire house that we'd lived in for many years—including Christopher's room and all his belongings. I can only imagine the strength it must have taken her to handle every last object, from his baseball cards and comic books to his sports and athletic trophies to all the letters and cards he'd saved from family, friends, and girlfriends over the years. How much of his clothing and other belongings should we keep? What should we donate or give away? Somehow, Alie found the answers to these torturous questions—a feat I doubt I could have accomplished if the task had fallen to me.

Oddly, Alie and I gave little thought to how I would run my business, how our eight-year-old daughter would adapt to a new school, or how we would stay close to our New Jersey–based family. We bought the house for the purpose of being in the best environment for our healing, and before we'd even moved in, it was clear that Delray Beach was going to do just that. I realized I could rely on my inner guidance, take responsibility for my choices, and trust that the path would reveal itself as I went along.

The Unique Bond of Siblings

Just as Alie and I were searching for a way forward after Christopher's death, Dani, too, had to find her own path. Around the time that we bought the house in Delray Beach, Dani decided to return to culinary school in Philadelphia. We'd been amazed when Dani had enrolled in culinary school, as she had a reputation in our household for burning toast, but she loved the program, with its classes on wine tasting and hotel and restaurant management. Like me, she believed that getting back to a familiar routine would be better for her than taking months off to sit around the house with nothing to do.

When a child dies, family and friends tend to focus on the parents' grief. The death of a child is unnatural, unexpected, and a parent's worst fear, and we are the recipients of the bulk of attention and concern. But the grief that siblings feel when one of them dies unexpectedly is hard to overstate. Siblings spend so much more time with *each other* than they do with almost anyone else—playing, talking, sharing, and even fighting. We cannot forget the loss and how deeply their lives are changed.

Dani and Christopher had the kind of sibling relationship where they could scream and throw things at each other, then be laughing together minutes later. As a teenager, Dani had often felt awkward and different from her friends. Christopher made her feel normal and accepted. The night of her eighth-grade dance, she came downstairs in her fancy dress and makeup, and Chris turned to Alie and said, "Mom, Dani looks *soooo* pretty." Dani later told me that was one of the first times in her life when she'd truly *felt* pretty. After all, if Christopher said it, it must be true.

The morning of Chris's last day on earth, which was his birthday, Dani had woken up to the sound of whispers coming from her bedroom doorway. It was Chris and Alex crouching together, both of them giggling as Chris coached Alex on what to say. "Say, 'Dani, wake uppppp!' Say, 'It's my birthdayyyy!'"

"It's my . . . I mean, hissss birthdayyyy!" Alex said. Dani immediately woke up laughing, and the three of them delighted in celebrating Chris's birthday. This was a classic example of their sibling bond.

Over the weeks and months since Dani had come to the hospital with us on that dreadful morning, she struggled to process the enormity of his death. Memories flooded into her head everywhere she looked. If she glanced in the direction of his bedroom, he'd be standing by his closet, picking out a tie, and asking her which one she liked better. Or he'd be sitting on the edge of his bed playing a video game, or reading, or waiting to ask her how her day was going. Every time she walked into the kitchen, she'd see him being silly with Alex, or picking up Alie and carrying her around the kitchen while she shrieked in delight.

Now, Dani would return to her life in Philadelphia profoundly changed. I wondered if her bond with Christopher would tug her to seek answers in spirituality, just as it was doing for me—if she would find her own inner pathway, just as I was being called to discover mine.

The Inner Pathway

As our move to Florida approached, I had plenty to occupy my mind. There were logistics to sort out, plans to make, and people to see and talk to. It would have been easy to distract myself with these everyday concerns and push away the deep questions that had become so important to me in the months since Chris died. But at this point, I had already stepped onto the inner pathway—or been thrust there, depending on how you looked at it—and there was no turning back. Those deep questions had taken on a central importance, and it would remain that way as long as I lived.

We all have inner dimensions of our lives—quiet and peaceful depths that are always accessible to us, if we know how to reach them. Our inner life gives us a bigger perspective on any circumstance occurring in our outer life. I found that there was always a bigger context from which to view life than from the obvious content we may be experiencing. The challenge for me was that my outer life was sometimes so loud and distracting that I could forget I even had an inner life. Between my busy office and my active family, it could sometimes seem like the outer world was all there was—until something reminded me it wasn't.

It became much easier to perceive my inner pathway when I learned to distinguish emotions from feelings. Emotions are passing reactions generated by the thought-based/intellectual portion of the mind. They may be pleasant or unpleasant, mild or intense, but they all take place on the surface level and will pass if you observe them with patience. Feelings take place at a deeper level and are not mixed with thought.

I knew that Chris's passing was so immense, unimaginable, and life-changing that it had to have a much higher purpose in my life than just to feel sorry for myself. I needed a bigger context for understanding this human tragedy. By tuning in to my feelings, this context began to reveal itself to me, little by little.

I was beginning to realize that Christopher's eternal spirit had never gone anywhere. It was still here, just as it was when it was housed in his beautiful earthly container. Christopher's human form certainly made it easier to see him and speak with him, but my true relationship with him was on a much higher level of consciousness: it was my spirit recognizing his spirit.

In my journal, I wrote,

> *Sometimes I wonder if we were together before this human life, because we are so close and so easily understood each other.*

This closeness is beyond the physical and mental and must be at a spiritual level that always was and always will be, before and after our human experience.

There must be a plan. This universe does not operate by mistake. Therefore, the plan for you was twenty-three years and seven hours in human form … but for eternity in the spiritual dimension?

Eternity in the spiritual dimension. It sounded right to me. Spirit to spirit, I was *always* with Christopher—whether I was in New Jersey or Florida, in a car or on a plane. Christopher's essence now dwelled only in that place of wholeness, and I could always meet him there.

Now, I just had to figure out how to access that place more often.

Chapter 3

What Is Reality?

Hey Brother,

What are my lessons to be learned from your death? They'd better be good ones, because this is too big and painful an event to not have a higher meaning. What is the reason for losing the human experience of being the father of a wonderful and loving son—a son with whom I had so much in common and who helped me see myself more clearly? I lost my human son and best friend and need to understand more.

I must open my mind to learn. Otherwise, this is all BS and I can get very angry and feel like all of this serves no purpose. Of course there have been some good times that have happened since you died, but there were so many good times before. I will always be your soulmate, but that was also already true—so why did you need to die?

Please help me understand. If there is a God, help me understand NOW.

Love forever and eternity,
Dad

AT THE END OF Alex's school year in June, we said goodbye to our house in New Jersey and moved into our new home in Florida. It felt good to settle into a new space, with palm trees in the backyard and sandy beaches just a few blocks away. Alex was excited about her new school, making new friends, and even living close to Disney World, a two-and-a-half-hour drive from Delray Beach; Alie joined the tennis club and was soon playing nearly every day.

But while the move to Florida gave Alie, Alex, and me a new lifestyle and environment, we were still very early in our grieving process, experiencing the raw emotions and having our many ups and downs on a regular basis. I could be gazing at the beautiful Florida sky at sunset, or taking a walk in our new neighborhood, and be overcome with a wave of sadness—or for that matter, a wave of missing him so much that tears would start flowing. Sometimes I had glimpses of clarity or even peace; other times, I found myself in a state of anguish, my yearning for answers to this mental turmoil so intense.

Grief doesn't stay behind when you move your residence. You are still who you are, and there is no running from the painful emotions; no physical move or change is going to make them go away. While I felt fortunate and knew that I was taking steps to move forward, it often felt like I was stepping backward first. In the space of a few hours, I could go from being angry at God to a place of higher understanding where I felt some degree of peace.

Sometimes, I would play a mental game in which I told myself that Chris was only gone for a while and that he would be returning—like when he went to college. It is so hard to accept the permanence of death—the fact that Christopher would never be physically walking in the door again. I knew that Alie and Alex were going through their own process of confronting this unimaginable fact, and I tried to support them as much as I could.

We were fortunate that we did not have to go through these agonizing times alone. Alie's mother moved into our old condo, and her father moved into a memory care home nearby; my father, Al, and my stepmom bought a condo in the same neighborhood, where they stayed part of the time. Twelve hundred miles away from our old home, we were still surrounded by close family with whom we could talk about Christopher.

During those early days in Florida, I went from being an avid reader to becoming an insatiable reader focused on books about healthy ways of grieving and books by authors who had also lost a child. I also read books about near-death experiences to understand what Chris may have gone through during his transition, and reading books by spiritual teachers became my passion, mission, and "friends." Authors like Eckhart Tolle and David Hawkins gave me new tools for engaging with my thoughts and emotions and the encouragement I needed to use them.

Tolle wrote, "Be willing to accept that things were supposed to happen the way they did, whether or not you can understand why […] You may not know where you're heading, but trust that you're being guided toward a place that serves you well."

Could I accept that Christopher was meant to live only twenty-three years? That his life, including its short duration, was perfectly designed for his journey? My thought-based mind told me I needed to find a reason I could understand, but what if there was a reason I *couldn't* understand? There are so many aspects of life that my human mind would never be able to fully grasp, but that didn't mean these dimensions of life didn't exist or had no meaning. In fact, it often meant the opposite: They contained a *higher* meaning that I could briefly access when the intellect of my mind settled down.

Eckhart Tolle's book *A New Earth* came out just a few months after Chris died. In my search for answers, I must have read it ten times. In *A New Earth*, Tolle asserts that life is always providing us with the experiences that contain the highest potential for our continued learning and the evolution of our consciousness at all times. "How do you know this is the experience you need?" he writes. "Because this is the experience you are having at this moment."

I pondered those sentences and others like them again and again. Sometimes, they made perfect sense. Other times, my mind rebelled. It was true that Christopher's death had heightened my commitment to my inner pathway; at the same time, it felt wrong to say that Christopher *needed* to die for this to happen. After all, couldn't we have explored this inner pathway together if he'd lived?

What Makes Love Real?

One day when I was sitting quietly with my journal, I began to reflect on the period of time between the moment when the police knocked on our door and the moment the nurse told Alie, Dani, and me that Christopher had died. During that interval, we had assumed that Christopher was still alive, and our relationship with him was unchanged other than the fear of what condition he may have been in. As we raced to the hospital, I felt the same love for him that I'd always felt. The strength of our bond was unchanged. I was only focused on seeing him, hugging him, loving him, and supporting him, no matter his condition. I didn't know that he had died, and therefore I continued to relate to him during this unknowing period "as if" he was still alive.

As I wrote about this unknowing period in my journal, I began to ask myself, what makes love real? Chris had already been gone from his human form for several hours when the police knocked on our door. But because I did not *know* that he had died, my relationship of love existed no differently for him during this time. Was the love I felt for Christopher during the drive to the hospital made any less real by the fact that he had already passed away? In other words, does love stop being real and/or able to be shared the moment a loved one dies?

It seemed obvious to me that to answer "yes" to these questions would be absurd. Christopher died at two in the morning, yet as we sat in the hospital waiting room at seven, I loved him just the same as I always had. If our love-based relationship had remained unchanged during the five-hour period that had elapsed between his death and our finding out about it, why would this wonderful feeling of love and joy that we shared have to change *after* this period?

Of course, it was extremely painful to accept that Chris and I would never have the fun and enjoyable human experiences that we shared as father and son, but I realized that the core of our relationship was unchanged by his death. We could have an ongoing and even growing relationship whether he was physically here or not. I didn't have to be sad every time I thought of him, because our relationship wasn't over.

Resistance and Acceptance

Over the weeks that followed, I kept asking myself the same question: Did Chris need to have a physical body in order for us to have an ongoing and growing love-based relationship? I was becoming more and more certain that he did not. Our relationships with departed loved ones might not *look* the same as our relationships with our loved ones who are still here. But that doesn't mean they aren't real. I could have a relationship with Chris based on the same love we'd always shared; it would just feel different on a sensory level than it had when he was in human form. We could no longer do the same things that we enjoyed when we were both in our human form, but we could *be* together.

It wasn't easy to stay open to this critical change in my understanding. My mind, with all its concepts and beliefs, pushed back. *Well, this all sounds nice*, it would say. *But I'll never see Chris again with my human eyes or hug Chris again with my human arms or be able to play golf with him again or be a grandfather to his children or watch him grow successful in his career.*

These objections were valid on the human level. After all, there is plenty to grieve in the loss of a person whose physical presence you cherished. Chris's journey as a human ended, and I missed him; it was as simple as that. But at the same time, it was true that my relationship with Chris had never changed, because that relationship was based in love, and love continues on even after death. I just needed to continually open myself to this new way of relating to him.

The love Chris and I share with each other *is* the reality of our relationship and will exist forever. Rather than drowning myself in sympathy or self-pity, I wanted the reality of this love-based relationship to grow and grow. I wanted to open myself up to new ways of communicating with Chris. For all I knew, he was communicating with me all the time, in ways I didn't yet understand. If Tolle was right, and this experience was perfectly designed for my continued growth and the evolution of my consciousness, wouldn't it be better if I dropped my resistance and learned to embrace this new life that was unfolding?

We Are Spiritual Beings

From the time I was a child, my father taught me that we are spiritual beings having a human experience. He used to say that the human part of our life is just a parenthesis between much vaster periods of spiritual life. In the months after Christopher's death, we spent hours discussing this idea, huddled together in the booth of a diner, with mugs of coffee in hand.

Many spiritual teachers say that death is a change of form and nothing to be feared. I knew how much I loved Christopher and how much he loved me. We had something special, the kind of close relationship that many people never get to experience at all. It seemed to me that in some very strange way, our relationship was even more special because we now got to experience a spiritual relationship while I remained in my human body and Christopher had departed from his. My focus now was to develop my awareness such that I could engage in this new level of our relationship fully.

When Chris was alive, I always loved talking to him. After he joined the firm, I looked forward to every evening when he'd get home after his appointments with clients. We'd sit around the kitchen table and debrief about the day. He'd tell me his opinions about the other new associates and ask for my advice about the business. Because he saw me as his dad and not "the boss," he could be honest with me in a way that few other people at my company could. I learned so much from these conversations, and they quickly became the high point of my day.

Was there some way to recapture the pleasure and meaning of those conversations, now that Christopher had left his human body behind? Was speech even necessary? After all, there are deeper levels of listening and understanding that go beyond mere speaking. When we talk with someone we love, or with anyone for that matter, the communication doesn't just take place at a verbal level but at the invisible dimensions of the intellectual, emotional, and feeling levels. In fact, a well-known 1960s study by Dr. Albert Mehrabian found that the spoken word accounts for as little as 7 percent of how we interpret what people are saying. The tone of voice, the intonations, the gestures, and the invisible world of vibrations and feelings account for the rest.

As much as I yearned to hear Christopher tell me about his day, I knew that our verbal conversations were just the surface interaction; underneath, there was a sea of connection whose vastness I had only begun to explore.

Searching for Signs

Those early months after Chris's death were filled with what felt like signs or messages from him. I would often take long walks and look up to the sky and the clouds. On numerous occasions, I saw formations that looked like two hearts intertwined, or I would see two clouds moving toward each other and feel that this was a sign. Other times, I would see someone who looked like Chris, or even see a car like his, and feel a sense of closeness with him. I also deeply yearned to have dreams about Chris, which happened often but not nearly as often as I would have liked.

On one occasion, Alie, Alex, Dani, and I all felt a strong sense of Chris's presence at the same time. Alie and I were sitting on our deck in Florida, waiting for Dani and Alex to get dressed so we could go out for dinner. We were all in our most dressy black outfits because we were headed to our favorite restaurant, City Oyster, a popular spot on Atlantic Avenue that was always humming with activity. Alie and I had just had a long and loving conversation about Chris, and I'd started to write in my black, hardcover journal. I looked up, and there was a beautiful all-black butterfly hovering over Alie. After a moment, it flew toward me and hovered under my chair. I put my finger out, hoping it would land on me, but it just flew around and then away.

Alie and I were captivated by this moment and felt a knowingness that Chris was with us. When we told Dani and Alex what had happened, they both said that they were writing and thinking about Chris at the same time we'd seen the butterfly. We felt so grateful to have had that visit with Chris. We went on to find out that Florida doesn't have any all-black butterfly species, and that made us feel even more strongly that something special had happened that evening.

One morning several months after Chris died, I went to a business conference where I was due to speak to a large group. I was thinking a lot about Chris and had a very strong feeling that he was present. After all, if he hadn't died, Chris would have been at this conference with me. I was about to leave my hotel room when I paused to glance at the emails on my Blackberry. I was stunned to see an email from Chris with the subject line "I'm back" and no other written words.

I went on to give my talk, invigorated by the feeling of Chris's presence. Afterward, I couldn't wait to get back to my Blackberry and see if there was another email. There were indeed additional emails from Chris, but unlike the first one, they didn't speak to me quite so directly. After a moment, I realized that the email I had seen that morning was from my *cousin* Chris, as were the subsequent ones. She'd been locked out of her account for a while and was writing to let me know that she "was back" online.

As I write this, I can still feel that warmth and feeling of closeness with Christopher that I experienced that morning. The feeling of his presence lingered, even after I'd realized the emails were from my cousin. Was this feeling real? Was Chris working through my cousin to send me a message? Or should I explain this away as a coincidence? After a while, I stopped looking for concrete yes-or-no answers to these questions and just appreciated the warmth, peace, and love that came from these instances of feeling close to Chris.

Christopher was no longer in a form that could communicate with me through speech, but did that make him any less real? Did reality only include those things that stimulated my senses—those things that I could see, hear, and hold with my hands—or did reality exist on a spiritual dimension?

What I *do* know is that the way we experience reality is subjective and solely based on how we choose to respond. Cultivating the reality of my ongoing and growing relationship with Chris was my choice to make.

What Is Reality?

As time went on, I kept asking myself, "What is reality?" Was it "really" Chris when a rare butterfly hovered over us, or when one of us had a dream about him? Was it real when I asked Chris a question in my journal and seemed to get a reply? When bereaved parents consulted psychics and channels to get messages from their deceased children, were *those* messages "real"?

Eventually, I realized that finding definitive answers to these questions wasn't all that important to me. I took comfort in those experiences, but for me, accepting life and the way it unfolds is the only reality. Life has been emanating from a Source for the fourteen billion years scientists say our universe has been here. Since I am *part* of this universal life, it makes sense to allow life to flow through me, without trying to control it. But while I can't change the flow of life, I can absolutely change how I choose to respond and therefore the way I *experience* my life.

We can't change the weather just because we don't like it, but we can accept rain as a necessary part of nature and not let it ruin our day. We can accept, adapt, and choose to experience whatever the weather may be with a loving and grateful attitude, no matter the circumstances. Similarly, we can't change the way someone is driving in front of us just because we don't like that they are going too slow. But we can choose to stay present and enjoy the ride. Through our God-given power of choice, we can choose to respond to any experience in our life in a healthy and accepting way.

One day, shortly after we'd moved to Florida, Alie and I took Alex to Disney World. We went on a simulated roller coaster where you sit in a seat in a dark room with a huge movie screen and speakers that provide all the sights and sounds of a real roller coaster. The only thing that's really moving is your seat, which tilts right and left and front and back. As the ride went on, I was struck by how real it felt. It was hard to believe we were just sitting in a room, not clicking up a steep roller coaster track, pausing at the top, then zooming down.

It seemed to me that my human experience was a lot like that simulated ride: it felt so real to my senses, yet it was only an illusion. I could get caught up in the ride's twists and turns, or I could realize it was only a simulation and enjoy the experience. While my thought-based mind was easily captured by the events of my life, my higher self was aware that these events were simply occurring, and I could observe them without fear.

My experience at Disney World felt like one more small turning point in the process of awakening. If outside events were more like a simulation, there was no need for resistance—but plenty of room for observing and choosing how I wanted to respond to my life. As I moved more and more toward letting go and allowing life to flow, I found myself becoming more compassionate and understanding of others and how they were experiencing the world. I would have conversations with people and find myself listening more, speaking less, and feeling more empathy toward them. While I still had my beliefs and opinions, I was doing my best to respect other people's choices as well. I knew they were all dealing with simulations of their own. I felt that I was becoming a kinder and more accepting human being thanks to Christopher and our growing relationship.

I was beginning to see beyond my initial reactionary thoughts, beliefs, and emotions and learning not to act on or blurt out what immediately came up. I reminded myself to look at the relationship I have with people at a spiritual level and respect them and their life and beliefs. Thoughts and emotions and even our physical senses tend to interpret information falsely and cause an initial wave or reaction. I needed to learn to respond from a bigger place, even if that meant leaving my own limited perspective behind—and this practice opened the next critical healing revelation for me.

Chapter 4

Seeing Death from Christopher's Side

To my beautiful son, Christopher,

As I look at your picture, I am amazed at your good looks, beautiful smile, bright eyes, and the love that comes through. I am also amazed that I am having this human experience of having lost a son. I am trying to understand (or make myself believe) that I have not "lost" a son but became more aware of a "spiritual partner," which is what we are in our essence.

You were born into a form called my son Christopher, and I have enormous gratitude for this twenty-three-year human experience. I would have liked it to be an experience which lasted for my entire human existence, but that was not the plan.

I am recognizing that it is not about my plan—it is about supporting you and your journey.

Love forever and eternity,
Dad

NOW THAT ALIE, ALEX, and my in-laws were settled into life in Florida, I began to commute to New Jersey by plane each week to continue running my business, leaving on the first flight out at six o'clock on Monday morning and returning on Friday afternoon. We purchased a condo on the Jersey shore where I could stay during the week, with a writing table overlooking the ocean where I could sit with my journal.

My life up until this point had been defined by work and family, going for long runs, and squeezing in whatever time I could for meditation and my spiritual interests. I was almost never alone. Now, for the first time, I found myself with hours of solitude in which to reflect, meditate, and write. With this new experience of alone time, I could devote more energy to my spiritual practice and give more attention to my inner path.

I also got to experience firsthand what it was like to live as a "bachelor." If I left dirty socks on my bedroom floor in the morning, they were still there when I got home from the office at night, and on top of that, the fridge didn't magically stock itself with food. But more importantly, a house was not a home for me without Alie's hug at the end of the day. Although I'd always valued and respected Alie's side of our traditional division of family responsibilities, I was reminded of just how much of our warm and comfortable and functional home life was due to her, and I felt even more gratitude for all that she did.

More and more, I began to think of Christopher as not only my son but my spiritual partner. Now that he was in spiritual-only form, our relationship was growing in ways that were very different than while he was on earth, and I was constantly seeking ways to keep on loving and supporting him. The idea of having a spiritual partnership with Chris inspired and motivated me far more than the other stories I could have told myself about his death—stories in which I was a father stuck in the depths of grief due to a tragic and unimaginable loss. When I thought of Chris as my spiritual partner, it seemed to me that while I had lost someone so special, I had also *gained* something: a best friend, a forever companion, and a love-based relationship on the other side.

When I was young, my father had taught me about what he called an "image." An image is a commitment to a purpose and vision that carries enormous power.

In one of my early journaling sessions in New Jersey, I set a strong image for my side of this spiritual partnership with Chris. I wrote,

> *I will study, contemplate, observe my life, and engage in discussions with insightful people until I increase my understanding and awareness to get to the point of "KNOWINGNESS" about our spiritual journey and relationship.*
>
> *My increased awareness of this higher level of consciousness will enable me to live a better life while human, and more naturally open up communication with you.*

In writing this image, I was acknowledging that I sometimes wondered if my ongoing relationship with Christopher was all in my head. I yearned to arrive at a place of knowingness where those doubts would be permanently eliminated. I needed to find a way to let go of these doubts—let go of listening to the push-back and skepticism of my mind. I knew I felt Chris's presence so strongly at times. What would it take to be in a place of knowingness more often?

Dani, Tieal, and I had each gotten a small heart-shaped tattoo they designed in memory of Christopher, shortly before they each went back to college. Sometimes, in the course of my busy days at the office, I would unbutton the cuff of my sleeve and run my thumb over it. In those days, it was unusual for a man working in finance to have a tattoo, so I kept it covered up by my shirt sleeve most of the time, but I liked to know it was there. It helped me feel Chris's presence. I could carry that with me in my interactions with others throughout my day. I would also share this feeling with my family. I hoped and wondered if Chris was in a spiritual partnership with them as he was with me.

Looking back, I can see that my alone time in our New Jersey condo was a critical incubator for my spiritual understanding to develop. It never would have occurred to me to carve out so much time alone, yet life had served up this experience for me, just when I needed it most. Thanks to this increased solitude, I could spend hours in quiet reflection, either writing in my journal or simply gazing at the sea, without feeling that I was being antisocial or neglecting anyone—or for that matter, overloading Alie with my intense desire to think and speak about Chris. I felt grateful to life for arranging this unexpected gift. Maybe there *was* something to Eckhart Tolle's claim that the experience we are having is the exact one we need in order to grow. If I could trust life to do exactly what was best for me in this moment, was it possible that life had been doing so all along?

Seeing Death from Christopher's Side

Slowly, I worked out the kinks in my part-time "bachelor" lifestyle. I arranged for the building's doorman to take care of my dry cleaning, and I ate my meals at the All Seasons diner, finding comfort in the familiar surroundings. Although some of my colleagues had worried that business would suffer when I moved to Florida, the opposite happened: everyone stepped up, and the company was thriving. I was starting to enjoy my work again, and I found that the time I was devoting to my inner pathway was making me a better boss: I was fully present, truly heard what people were saying, and found it easier to allow creative solutions to be discovered.

Creative ideas and flashes of insight were also coming to me more frequently in my journaling. Now that the initial shock of Christopher's death was behind me, I found myself asking more questions and expressing more curiosity, or simply following my stream of consciousness and seeing where it led me. One evening, I was sitting at my writing table with my journal when it occurred to me that I could look at Chris's death from his side. Until now, I'd been more focused on my own experience—my sadness, grief, and yearning to see him. But what about Chris? Maybe for him, death was part of his ongoing spiritual journey—the completion of the beautiful trajectory of his human experience. Maybe from his perspective, it wasn't a tragedy at all, but a natural and orderly progression. Why should his experience of death be defined by the pain it caused me?

When this idea came to me, it started out as a subtle awareness. I kept this insight to myself, turning it over in my mind again and again, letting it marinate. Over time, it grew into a major shift in my perspective. If I could look at this experience from *his* side instead of just mine, it could change everything. Just contemplating that new paradigm felt like a small release from the grip of grief.

Had Christopher's life journey been perfectly designed, including his death at age twenty-three? Maybe it had—and the only mistake that existed was in my mindset, not in the reality of what had happened. I struggled with the primary and essential idea that we live in a perfect universe. My mind came up with countless reasons why Christopher's death was a mistake. It was hard to stay open to the idea that if it happened, it was supposed to happen. But when I refocused my attention, a larger understanding continued to dawn on me. After all, nature was perfect, with its graceful flowers and beautiful trees, the majestic ocean, and the orderliness of the universe. If these levels of reality were perfect, how could any level of life in this universe be mistaken or flawed?

As this expanded perspective took root and grew stronger, I found that I had more options for how I could respond to my strong emotions and their accompanying thoughts. I could either be centered on how this experience related to me only, or I could be more aware and open to Chris's side—and to the perfection of a universe in which every falling leaf, snowflake, and ocean wave could not have happened any other way.

The Gift of Uncertainty

As I slowly opened myself to seeing life in a new way, I realized there was, in fact, very little that I could say I fully understood or knew. Far from being a source of anguish, however, I found that there was a level of peace in this unknowingness.

Many times, I would look up at the stars in the sky at night, or gaze at a tree growing in its unique way from the earth, or contemplate almost anything in nature, and realize how little I understood about the processes of life. As humans, we give things labels like "an oak tree" or "a weed" or "the sun and the sky and the Milky Way." Just because we've named them, we think we know them; we mistake our thoughts about things for their true nature. But when we pause to truly contemplate these wonders, they are revealed as complex, mysterious, and awe-inspiring, impossible to contain within our mental concepts that, by design, are limited. How much more fulfilling it is to be curious in the face of these mysteries than to claim that we *know*!

I was beginning to see that my mind struggled to hold a large enough context or view of life. I would watch my mind be drawn to concepts, beliefs, and opinions, but not naturally drawn to the larger "whole." It seemed to me that my intellectual mind was always giving me incomplete answers based on what was already stored in my mind. Likewise, my own experience of life was just one piece of a much larger whole.

When I thought of Christopher's death from my own side, I could only feel the pain. But when I focused on Chris's side, it created space where I could love and support him on his journey. The depth of my commitment to this new perspective was brought home to me one day when a good and well-meaning friend called me on the phone.

"Steven," he said, "I was speaking with an attorney friend of mine, and I told him what happened to Chris. He said there's no question you have a wrongful death lawsuit on your hands that would settle for millions. I can give you his number if you'd like."

By that point, I had already progressed far enough on my inner pathway that the suggestion of a lawsuit felt very wrong. I was not and have never been litigious, and I was certainly not interested in making someone pay for Chris's death. Focusing on the circumstances of his passing would go completely against my mission of seeing the larger context, keeping a curious mindset, and allowing space for uncertainty. And I would not even consider subjecting my family and myself to that torturous process. While lawsuits may have a place in society, it was not my purpose or place to focus on blame. It wouldn't change the fact that Christopher was gone.

While I appreciated my friend's point of view, I declined his offer without hesitation. I was embracing my real purpose more and more every day, and the one thing I *did* know for sure was that Christopher's death had a much higher meaning in my life. I needed to stay laser-focused on this meaning, which was easier to hold in my awareness when I looked at this experience from his side.

Supporting Christopher's Journey

The more I accepted seeing death from Christopher's side, the more I realized that I could be a source of love and support for him as he continued his journey instead of withdrawing into my own grief and pain. Truly loving someone means that you support them in all they choose to do. During Christopher's time in human form, I supported his decisions, even when they ran contrary to what I would do. Why should I stop supporting him now?

I remembered the time close to his high school graduation when he turned down a full soccer scholarship to an excellent university. As a father, I'd been excited about this university pursuing him as well as him being a college athlete; not only that, but Chris loved soccer, and this scholarship would have covered his tuition. I couldn't understand why he would pass up the opportunity to play a sport at which he excelled, and at a college level.

"Dad," he explained, "I don't want to beat up my body over the next four years. My friends who are college athletes have all kinds of injuries—some that could affect them for life. Besides, I'm not good enough to ever play in the pros as a career, and I'm not even sure I would want to anyway."

When Chris explained this, it all made sense. I could set aside my disappointment at not being "the star soccer player's dad." Instead, I could focus on Chris's wisdom and maturity in looking down the road and making the decision that fit him best. Whether or not I agreed with his decision, I could see that it was a good and meaningful one. If I could support him in this way at that time, why not continue to do so after he died?

When I looked at my thought process, it went something like this:

- Christopher died in an auto accident.
- The fact that this occurred must mean it was meant to occur, because life happens perfectly. There can be no accidents in this universe.
- I love and support Christopher unconditionally; therefore, I choose to look at this experience from his side, stop asking why, and support his journey.
- Moving beyond "why" allows the looping thoughts to subside and opens space for healing to occur.
- My power comes from my ability to choose how I respond, and my choices determine how I experience the flow of life.

Seeing death from Chris's side became a new mindset I was building, and it was slowly but steadily changing my experience of grieving. Now, when someone gave me their condolences, while I appreciated and understood where they were coming from, I would remember with gratitude that Christopher was pursuing his journey on the other side. Remembering this gave me a feeling of peace. When I thought about it this way, how could I be anything but happy for him? I felt it was a miracle that I could maintain this level of love and support for Chris, even though I still did not agree with the fact that he had died.

One night, I had dinner with a good friend of mine whom I had known for over thirty years, whose wife had died of cancer six months before. I had always looked up to him and considered him a mentor.

"Steven, I still feel so strange that people are going about their lives as usual, while mine has been turned upside down," he told me.

I felt comfortable enough to ask, "Have you tried looking at it from Karen's side?"

"What do you mean?" he said.

I explained that from Karen's point of view, it was entirely possible that her human death was just a transition in a much larger experience that he and I couldn't fully comprehend. It wasn't just that she had been released from the physical suffering of cancer; she had entered a new dimension and continuation of life and learning. *We* were the ones who were hurting. What would happen if we looked beyond our own pain?

I'll never forget my friend's reaction. He looked stunned, like a deer in headlights. Slowly, he sat back in his chair. With a confused but curious look on his face, he said, "Seeing it from Karen's side. I never thought about that."

I could see a lightbulb turning on in his head. For the rest of the evening, he had a lighter feeling about him and seemed to find some joy in the idea that he still could, and should, support Karen in her journey. I wondered how many more people's lives would be changed if they began to relate to their departed loved ones in this expanded way.

Trusting the Plan

Even as I was having these profound insights during my time in New Jersey, my favorite moment of the week was walking out of the terminal of the Palm Beach International Airport and seeing Alie and Alex waiting for me in the bright sunshine. "Daddy!" Alex would shriek, running toward me for a hug. Alie and I would spend the weekend going to Alex's swim meets, or taking her to the white sand beach that was just a few blocks from our home. Alex was a little quieter and shyer than Dani and Christopher had been, and sometimes Alie and I worried that Christopher's death had caused her to withdraw. But when I saw her fearlessness and motivation in the pool, and the way she bonded with the other kids on her swim team, I knew that she, too, was growing and learning after the experience.

Sometimes, when I looked at Alex, I felt a pang of sadness or even anger at the way life had gone. My beautiful daughter didn't deserve to go through this big of a loss at such a young age. It pained me that she had to grow up without the inspiration and protection of the older brother who'd always been there for her. But when I reminded myself to start from the premise that everything happens for a purpose, contained within an all-encompassing universal plan, this allowed me to stop asking why and choose to respond with more openness to the journeys that we were all on.

I could be okay with not having to feel that I knew. I could be comfortable in a world I didn't control, in which I didn't have all the answers, and which felt unpredictable. I could choose to believe that life is designed to teach me and provides me with the perfect opportunities to learn and grow. The other alternative was to believe that life was designed to *torture* me—and what was the use of that?

Around this time, I began to attend a weekly spiritual class based on the book *A Course in Miracles*. *ACIM*, as it is commonly referred to among students, is a spiritual book that was published anonymously in 1975 and later attributed to Dr. Helen Schucman, a clinical psychologist at Columbia University. It teaches the importance of awakening to the presence of love in your life through a process of forgiveness and shifting to a place of knowledge rather than thought. *A Course in Miracles* appealed to me because I felt that my real and higher purpose during my human experience was to transform myself from using my thought-based/intellectual mind, which carried fear and judgment, to living from my more natural caring, loving, and compassionate self.

One day, a member of the group asked about how to deal with the many appalling current events occurring in our world. The very aware and insightful spiritual teacher, Joe Tedesco, replied in his no-nonsense way: "The world just keeps worlding on." I think about these words often. While we may not control all the twists and turns that life throws at us, and certainly not all that goes on in the world, the way I experience my life is determined by the way I respond—no matter what the world is doing.

Life will do what it does. This is a fundamental truth, yet so hard for us humans to grasp. We think that if we wish hard enough, or reason hard enough, or do all the right things, or try to manipulate everything going on around us, we will somehow gain control of life and be happy—when really, the only power we have is over our own reactions. For a long period after Chris died, my intellectual mind had tried desperately to reshape reality, imagining scenarios in which his death wouldn't have happened. The more I accepted life as it was, these futile attempts began to fade away.

I realized the activity of my mind was like waves crashing on a beach. The first wave that came in response to a certain event was often filled with emotions or even drama. I learned that this first wave came from what the psychiatric community would consider the subconscious mind: the part that holds all of our beliefs, opinions, judgments, and stored habits. I would discipline myself to just watch that wave and not react. Often, I found that the next wave or waves behind the first big one were usually more manageable, and I had a better chance of choosing how to respond. Slowing myself down was the key.

When I let the initial emotional waves subside, I could see that Chris's journey during his human experience was designed, and must have only needed to be, twenty-three years. This was so difficult to accept, but it was the truth of what had happened. I could resist it, I could hate it, I could be forever angry and keep suffering the rest of my life, or I could accept that this was his journey, see it from his side, and support him in his experience.

The way I related to Chris's journey would determine how my journey would move forward—and I had better choose wisely, because life still had a lot of surprises in store for me.

Chapter 5

Embracing What Can Be

Hey Chris,

Sometimes, I still can't believe that you are not here in human form. I understand more than ever how love and relationships continue to grow, even after death. Love is at a spiritual level, and goes on forever.

Because of you, I have become so much more aware that I am a spiritual being, and I thank you for this amazing gift. I am now enjoying, and have begun to cherish, the awareness of our spiritual relationship.

I love you. My humanness misses you so very much. But my spirit knows that nothing has changed except that our awareness of each other now takes place at a much deeper level. Let's keep helping each other grow in consciousness.

Love forever and eternity,
Dad

SPLITTING MY TIME BETWEEN Florida and New Jersey had another priceless benefit: I got to spend some weekends one-on-one with Dani in Philadelphia, just a one-hour drive from my condo on the Jersey shore. The time Dani and I spent together gave us an opportunity to build our relationship in a way that might not have happened otherwise. Dani was just coming out of her teenage years, and as any parent knows, there's a wide range of differences and disagreements that can come up during this sensitive time.

Things didn't always go as smoothly as we would have liked during these years, mostly because Dani and I are so similar: We're both strong-willed and have strong opinions, and that could cause us to butt heads. But the love that we have as father and daughter has always prevailed. We were now finding ourselves in a blossoming adult relationship, accelerated by our need for each other's support during this agonizing and emotional time in our lives.

On Saturday mornings when I was in New Jersey, I'd have a leisurely cup of coffee on the deck of my condo, stare at the ocean for a while, then drive to Philly in time to meet Dani for lunch. She'd choose from one of the many great restaurants in Philly, where the waiters, waitresses, and kitchen staff were often her friends from culinary school. After lunch, we'd take long walks through the city or along the river, reminiscing about Christopher and having discussions that were truly therapeutic for both of us during these difficult months.

Dani had taken a keen interest in her own spiritual path since Chris's passing, reading many books and talking with her friends at college who had been through similar experiences and were also seeking answers. Often, we'd spend hours in a bookstore, pointing out books and authors to one another. Dani introduced me to the work of Thich Nhat Hanh, as well as the excellent book *Many Lives, Many Masters* by Brian Weiss, which influenced me so much. We would discuss Buddhism and its many principles as well as subjects like near-death experiences and where Chris might be on his journey. We traded notes on what we were reading and what we planned to read next.

Dani also had many dreams about Chris, including lucid dreams, that were so wonderful to hear about. One day on our walk she shared, "Dad, I had a lucid dream last night where Chris and I were sitting together. I knew I was dreaming, and it felt so good to be with Chris, and I just kept hugging him because I knew I could. That was all I wanted to do. He started sharing his thoughts with me, and he looked directly at me and said, *Always be a student*. And then I woke up." With tears in both of our eyes, we felt the significance of his wise advice that has made an impact on both of our lives. I enjoyed our deep discussions thoroughly and always looked forward to the next visit.

This period was a powerful time in our growth, both individually and in our relationship, and I will always be grateful that Dani and I had this one-on-one time together. All these years later, we both realize how fortunate we were, during those very difficult and sad times, that our shared interest in spirituality helped strengthen our bond. My whole life, I had felt that my father was the person who literally woke up my soul thanks to his dedication as a spiritual seeker. I hoped I was playing a similar role for Dani as she searched for answers in the wake of Christopher's death.

Discovering What Can Be

Sometimes, spending time with Dani and learning more about her life and aspirations would lead me to daydream about what Chris's life would have been like if he had lived. He would have gotten married and had children; Alie and I would be grandparents; he would have continued to be in business with me and eventually taken the reins of the company; we would have enjoyed countless holidays, birthdays, and our daily conversations. I could start to feel sad and regretful, thinking of all the things that could have been and now would never be.

But, one day, on that ride home from Philly, while watching all these thoughts flow through my mind, a lightbulb turned on. It dawned on me that if I focused more on Chris's ongoing spiritual journey, and less on what could have been, I could feel hopeful and even excited about what could still be in our relationship.

When I let myself go down the road of what *could have been* with Chris, my mind manufactured scenes and stories with no basis in reality. It started to feel like I'd been deprived of all these wonderful, imaginary experiences, and I could even get very angry. But when I reframed my focus on *what could be*, it opened space for me to see opportunity. My relationship with my son wasn't over; on the contrary, I had been gifted with a spiritual partnership that was enabling me to grow in understanding like never before.

So what could still be? A beautiful and growing spiritual partnership; a window into a more peaceful dimension within myself; a link to my son that was made of pure feeling, unshackled by thought. Whereas before, my relationship with my son had been characterized by memorable outside experiences, this new relationship would depend on the qualities I cultivated on the inside. I felt that Chris's spiritual "only" journey had just begun, maybe like Dani's spiritual journey that she was just discovering. I would participate in both of their journeys, just in different ways. And both would have a profound effect on my growth.

When I journaled, it felt like Christopher and I were spending time together—like he was there. Because Chris and I were together during this time, I found myself only wanting and able to write from my highest truth. Writing seemed to come more directly from feeling, whereas communicating through speech can sometimes get caught up in our thoughts. I was not going to write about what was going through my head but focused instead on what was going through my heart. Anything less than this would have been a waste of time—and I was not going to waste any time when I was with Chris.

Of course, the biggest difference in communicating with Chris through my journal was that when responses came, they were in the form of deeper feelings. It could be a wave of calmness or peace, sometimes more clarity, and other times a feeling of closeness or love far beyond the level of emotion. Because my mind was quiet and focused, I could differentiate these feelings and embrace them in their fullness, without being distracted by mental chatter.

While there is no question that it was much easier, and more fun, to communicate with Chris when he was in his physical body, this quieter and subtler form of communication had quickly become deeply meaningful to me. My journaling sessions with Chris became a daily ritual I so looked forward to and were every bit as precious to me as the evening catch-up conversations we had enjoyed when he was alive.

Finding Love Within

My journaling sessions with Chris taught me that love isn't a thing we receive, but a state of being we uncover. When I journaled with Chris, I felt profound love; and yet Chris wasn't "there" to give love back to me. Instead, the love I felt was internal, and as I shared it with Chris, it grew even more—it had nothing to do with being "returned."

I realized that sharing my love makes the feeling stronger. This might be why it's so easy to mistakenly believe that love comes from some outside person, place, or thing. In fact, love comes from the inside. The love we feel is the love that already lives inside of us; we may be awakened to its presence by another person, but they didn't put it there. The love we have inside is like an endless pile of gold; when another person shines a flashlight on the gold, we sometimes think they put it there, when really they're just shining the light so we can see what was there all along.

This realization had a profound effect on all my love-based relationships. Knowing that my inner capacity for love was endless and ever present, I became less dependent on looking for love and affection from others and more focused on sharing my love. If I could feel tremendous love for Chris without "receiving" anything in return, why should I bring the expectation of a certain response to my relationships with other people in my life?

Christopher's death had already taught me that my *relationships* with the people I love exist on the inside and can be felt and nurtured whether they are far or near and whether I speak to them out loud with my voice or silently within the stillness of my heart. Now, I was learning that *all* of my love existed within, and it was my choice at all times to share it or not. This gave me a sense of happiness and security unlike any I had known before.

Observing, and the Seduction of Sadness

Even as I was developing an expanded awareness of *what could be* in my relationship with Chris, my mind would still occasionally send up a flurry of resistance: *An ongoing relationship is impossible. You're imagining it. You're in denial.* I worried that I was using spirituality to comfort myself or to avoid facing the hard truth that Christopher was gone forever. It was also true that I was by no means finished with the process of grieving.

I remember one day when I was at home in New Jersey, I was looking out the window in my sunroom, having a strong wave of sadness and missing Christopher. I allowed myself to feel this emotion as I cried intensely, but as I just watched and felt, I slowly began to realize that the sadness could not kill me. This sadness was not me, but was just passing through me. As I moved forward with my day, the sadness seemed to evaporate back to wherever it came from. The key for me was that I did not give this emotion any more energy by dwelling on it, adding to it, discussing it with anyone, or creating stories or drama around it. I just observed it and felt it.

Over the course of my subsequent reading and study, I noticed how many spiritual authors emphasized the importance of becoming the observer of one's thoughts and emotions, as opposed to identifying with them. I decided to take up this practice in earnest. When I took the position of observer, I realized that all of the incessant babbling going on in my head couldn't possibly be me because of the very fact that I was the one observing it. I could watch thoughts and emotions flow through my mind and body, and while I still felt them, I did not have to react to them. There was a small but critical space between me and them. Observation meant adding nothing to the experience, not even a single thought or opinion, and allowing the sadness to just be.

After experiencing countless periods of deep sadness, I knew that it would come, and it would go, if I chose not to dwell in it. As I practiced observing the sad feelings without engaging with them in any way, I became aware of an interesting phenomenon: some part of me was *attracted* to the sadness, maybe even wanted to experience more of it. There was a strange temptation to draw it out by engaging in stories and fantasies, feeling sorry for myself, or even looking for someone who would bond with me in this sadness and provide sympathy. There was a peculiar comfort in this sadness, even though I knew it was not a good place for me.

The moment I gave in to one of these unproductive choices, the feeling of sadness would move from my gut, where I could handle it, to my head. Instead of being a physical sensation, the sadness would mix with thoughts, which could then spin stories out endlessly and create suffering. It didn't matter that these thought-based stories were made up and gave me no relief; my mind just wanted to go back into thinking mode to feel in control, regardless of how bad the suffering could become.

My other choice was to embrace the sadness, feeling it fully with no fear. This was difficult at times because the sadness could be so intense. Sometimes, I could only stay with it for a few moments at a time before my thought-based mind would take over again. The more I practiced taking the position of observer, my ability to stay with the sadness in its pure form increased. Instead of converting the sadness into thoughts, I could feel its pain without turning away. Pain was manageable because I knew it would pass through me, and I was learning to let it go. Sadness, like most emotions, is overrated, and I did not have to worry that it could crush me.

Feeling the sadness fully allowed it to burn itself out, like a piece of charcoal, whereas if I mixed it with thought, it would keep on burning. Thought has a tendency to keep looping over and over, endlessly expressing itself rather than releasing its energy; feeling deeply sets us free. When I experienced this release, it brought me back to a place of lovingness where I felt close to Christopher again.

Living from the Inside Out

The position of observer was a much more pleasant and empowering place from which to live my life. This natural state was always within reach—yet there were so many outside distractions that grabbed my attention, I could easily forget and fall back into reactive habits. The more I practiced staying in the observer position, the easier it became to choose not to engage with the chatter. The natural outcome of this choice was that I felt my deeper and calmer inner self emerging.

Now that this shift was occurring, I found that looking outside of myself for happiness no longer worked. While nice cars, nice houses, money in the bank, great vacations, and even friends and family can provide a temporary feeling of happiness or security, they contained the potential for loss due to their temporary nature. People could die; places could change; things that were so valuable one day could get old and outdated. When we live from the outside in, we are subject to all the pain, fear, and disappointment that comes from the temporary nature of these pleasures. However, when we live from the inside out, focusing on the quality of our awareness and enjoying the experience of the present moment, we can enjoy all of the pleasures of life while experiencing deep peace all the time, no matter what's going on in the outside world.

I wanted to live more of my life in this quieter place. I began to seek out short periods during the course of my busy day to slow things down—to cool my jets, so to speak. I realized that my real self was distinct from the roles I played throughout the day, whether that be businessman, colleague, or even father or husband. My *real* self was still, calm, and based in love, which is my essence—always there no matter where I was or what I was doing.

I would always keep a higher consciousness book by one of my favorite authors in the briefcase I brought to the office. Throughout the day, I'd pull it out and read a sentence or two. It felt like a friend who helped me stay balanced. Sitting at my desk, I'd take a few breaths to let the message sink in. Even though I valued my role as CEO in my growing business and played it to the best of my ability, I knew that this was not my true identity. I could observe myself going about my tasks and thinking my thoughts while remaining conscious that underneath it all, I was something far greater: I was a spiritual being.

Over time, my practice of being the observer led to a complete shift in how I experienced reality. It felt that the real me, the observer, was living in a little protected space somewhere near the base of my neck, watching all that was going on, including whatever I was saying and doing. Many times, coming from this space enabled me to be more sharply aware of all that was unfolding around me, stay present, and use my power of choice more wisely, all while wrapped in a deep sense of calm.

I had to continually remind myself that I am, in fact, a spiritual being having this human experience and therefore have so much more depth of feeling than emotion. Allowing myself to live my life from my higher self is as close to truth and love as I would ever get. But to open space for this, I needed to turn down the volume on my thinking/intellectual mind more often.

Turning Down the Volume

I found that managing the amount of mental stimulation in my life was becoming very important. Whether it was phone calls, text messages, emails, social media, TV, the news, or any other distractions that seemed to steal my attention, I needed to be more vigilant of what I allowed in. Choosing how many of these things to allow into my world was my responsibility, and turning away from them required some discipline. These powerful stimuli can eat away at our ability to be present and attuned to our feelings. While I wasn't going to give up these media, as they are very useful, I realized I had to manage them more effectively if I was going to stay tuned in to my higher self more of the time.

When I was at home in Florida or traveling to business conferences, I decided to be more intentional about taking walks, spending time in nature, and finding time to read spiritual books, write in my journal, and listen to spiritual talks online. Sometimes, when Alie, Alex, and I got home from one of Alex's swim meets or a trip to the beach, I'd sit on the back porch. I'd watch the palm trees swaying and the clouds drifting by and listen to the birds singing without *doing* anything at all. When I took the time to simply enjoy the pleasure of existence, it felt so much better than engaging in the compulsive mental chatter that the wrong kind of stimuli could so easily activate in me.

Every day, I would take time to meditate, sitting alone in a quiet room. I would focus my mind either on my breathing or on a simple mantra, and this had the effect of creating a space apart from my incessant thinking. Over the course of many meditation sessions, I began to find the place that spiritual teacher Gary Zukav calls the Seat of the Soul and other teachers sometimes call the Higher Self, Holy Spirit, or countless other names.

All these years later, the practice of meditation remains very helpful to me for turning down the volume of life. Mental chatter can still come through when I meditate, but I can choose to watch it rather than engage with it. I can then bring myself back to my mantra or breath and return to my peaceful place. Meditation gave me the extraordinary realization that engaging with thoughts, opinions, and judgments is what gives them energy and life; they have no life of their own. The more

I practiced these skills in meditation, the more I began to use them in my everyday life.

Understanding that it was totally *my choice* to engage or not engage with thoughts, judgments, and opinions passing through my mind was huge. These things could *only* exist when I shined the light of my consciousness on them; instead, I could shine that light on the present moment and allow life to flow without resisting it. In order to give myself a visual, I would imagine I had a miner's hard hat on with a head light on the front that I could turn the light in an entirely different direction and "light up" another choice. As the observer, I had absolute freedom of choice in how to direct my awarencss. I would soon discover just how life-changing this power could be.

Chapter 6

All of Our Power Is Beyond Thought

Hey Chris,

I love you so very much. I am starting to understand that all love is within. I want to know—really know—more about this "formless" dimension of which we are all a part.

The physical and mental aspects of my life can be loud and distracting, but they are nothing compared to the vast, calm, and clear realm of the spiritual dimension where we all have our source and I feel our spiritual partnership will eternally be together.

Remembering to allow life to flow through me is so important. And observing this human experience of senses, thought, and emotion from my higher self feels much more peaceful. Fear, worry, and sadness can still be felt, but pass through me much more easily as I am learning not to engage thought with them. Awakening to my reality as a spiritual being while living this human life is my absolute purpose, and you are my window. Thank you.

Love forever and eternity,
Dad

IN MY ONGOING QUEST to live more of my life from my higher self, I began to work one-on-one with Joe Tedesco, who ran the *Course in Miracles* study group near our home in Florida. Joe's life included the military, being a policeman, and building a successful contracting business as an entrepreneur. When he stumbled on the book *A Course in Miracles* almost thirty years ago, he devoted himself to its principles and it started his spiritual awakening.

Although now only in his fifties, he was retired and would take time to coach people who were serious in their spiritual journey. A caring, loving, and affable man with glasses and a tiny soul patch on his chin, he was also straightforward and direct in both his lectures and coaching on the importance of choosing love over fear—and how this choice could profoundly transform our experience of the world. In one of our first private sessions together, I shared a very personal and concerning issue going on in my life, and he gave me advice I will never forget.

"Steven," he said, "whenever you find yourself faced with a challenging person or situation, ask yourself one question: 'What would love do now?'"

I found that when I could quiet my mind and ask this question, it had the effect of opening me up to a range of responses that would not have occurred to me otherwise. By aligning myself with the perspective of love, as opposed to old habit patterns and judgments from my ego, I more naturally gravitated toward words, actions, and choices based on compassion. My focus on my little self and my narrow needs was not as strong, and I could see a course of action that was truly benevolent for all parties involved.

Working with Joe as my spiritual coach was wonderful. I loved having one-on-one guidance, even though I could feel intimidated at times due to his intense Zen style and his total commitment to dealing in absolute truth with no excuses accepted. That being said, he was also a nonjudgmental sounding board to whom I could express my fears and insecurities as well as ask my endless questions about awakening to my spiritual reality. I left every session feeling even more inspired to keep following my inner pathway, and the doubts I'd carried at times about my commitment to my spiritual growth began to fade away.

One of the first answers I got from the question "What would love do now?" came in the form of a gift "given" by Chris. A couple months before Alie, Alex, and I moved to Florida, I'd attended Tieal's graduation from Lynn University—a bittersweet day, as Tieal was still in deep grief and shock over Christopher's death. Afterward, Alie and I had a long conversation about Tieal. We talked about how she was like another daughter to us and how we would always be there for her, and we thought about all the ways Christopher would have wanted to celebrate this milestone in her life. Chris and Tieal were so committed to each other, and Chris was already preparing to be the provider in their lives. Tieal was one of six sisters, and she and Chris looked forward to building their own large and loving family someday. Now, Tieal was on her own, without the love of her life, and needed to start her life with loans, no car, and having to move back home.

Chris had some money saved in a bank account, and Alie and I knew that his dream was to buy Tieal a car as soon as he could. This was another moment where Alie and I looked at each other and knew that the only right thing to do was to make Chris's dream come true. Alie and I found the perfect new SUV for her, paid for it with Chris's savings, and gave her the car as a belated graduation present. She was so surprised and grateful beyond words. All the three of us could do was give each other a long and emotional hug, during which we all felt Chris's presence very strongly.

Guided by the Heart

I had many more opportunities to use my newfound tool of asking, "What would love do now?" both in my business and my personal life. In my role as CEO of a financial services company, I dealt with many sensitive situations that had potentially high-impact consequences. When dealing with tough employee relationships, making decisions that would affect so many, or even guiding advisors with an unhappy client, asking this critical question rebalanced me and opened my mind to more creative solutions. Even in situations where it felt like there was no good answer, when I asked myself, *What love would do now?* I found the words that seemed to raise everyone involved to a higher level where better options appeared.

Another role I enjoyed was that of board member. One day, I was attending a board meeting at the private elementary school, Oak Hill Academy, from which Christopher had graduated in New Jersey. After Christopher's death, Alie and I had worked with Oak Hill to establish the Christopher Ferrara Giving Wall, a beautiful memorial housed in the school's student activities center, the donations from which would fund new and needed improvements on campus. In addition, we created an annual scholarship with OHA called the Christopher Ferrara Spirit Award, given to the child who exemplified caring and concern for others, a positive and giving attitude, and school spirit. Staying involved with the school as a board member was one more way for me to give back and ensure that other kids had the same opportunity to be guided in their character development and growth into responsible adults as I felt Christopher experienced there.

In this particular meeting, the board was discussing delicate situations involving parents who were way behind in paying their child's tuition and taking advantage of other rules the school had in place. It had gotten to the point where some board members were arguing that these children should no longer be allowed to attend the school. The discussion was going around and around in circles, with some members pointing out that not paying tuition was clearly not an option and other members expressing reluctance to remove a child from school due to the parents' mistakes or bad behavior.

I asked myself the question, "What would love do now?" and let it marinate quietly in my mind. It quickly became clear to me that love was *not* on the side of kicking a child out of school due to their parents' mistakes. I also felt a growing sense of love and compassion for all the people involved: the students, the parents, and even my fellow board members. When it was my turn to speak, I spoke from the heart: I told them I fully recognized the school contract and rules. They were clear that a student could be expelled if tuition fees were unpaid or rules were broken. However, as a board, we had the ability and responsibility to be more creative in our approach to solutions. Our priority was to do our very best to ensure that each child had every opportunity to learn and grow.

I made a few suggestions, including that the board meet with the parents and discuss the need and reason for rules, and suggested that we could develop a payment plan that would help the delinquent parents catch up with the tuition. We could even show them how to apply for a student loan or a grant while allowing their child to complete their education.

As I spoke, I noticed many people at the table nodding in agreement—even the ones who had been arguing with one another just minutes before. This started up a productive, creative, and positive discussion. By asking myself, "What would love do now?" I aligned with my higher, more compassionate self, and it had the effect of moving everyone present toward a more caring and empathetic place. This clearer mindset that we all felt seemed effortless, as opposed to the thoughts in which we were all entangled just moments before. A decision was made that resulted in better understanding parents, children who could continue their private school education, and the school not breaking its boundaries.

I realized that when I came from this place of higher awareness, even the most complex problems with so many moving parts could be resolved effortlessly, in a way my intellectual mind could never have accomplished. This new perspective connected me to a more loving, caring, and inclusive way of moving forward.

Choosing the Right Tools

I began to feel a sense of excitement about the flow and congruency with which my mind could operate. I was amazed by how much I could accomplish from this place of creativity. I began to literally see the world in a different way. While my intellect was a reliable workhorse for accomplishing specific tasks and for planning, my new mindset of openness, asking for guidance, and not having to have all the answers made me feel capable of reaching into a higher level of consciousness.

I recognized that thoughts have limited power to provide answers to the deep questions that arise as we confront life's challenges. When confronted with a force as life-changing as the grief I felt after Christopher's death, I knew I needed access to much more awareness than my ordinary thoughts could offer. Yet, I would find myself struggling with letting go. I would put more and more pressure on my thought-based mind to give me answers, of which it was simply incapable. This only had the effect of generating the same looping thoughts over and over. I reminded myself often that access to higher dimensions of awareness, consciousness, and energy can all be found within the vastness of my mind when I quieted my thoughts.

In *The Power of Now*, Eckhart Tolle writes that nothing exists but the present moment. The present moment is our only point of contact with reality; everything else is a mind-manufactured illusion. Tolle tells us that when we think, we project ourselves into the past or future, losing that point of contact in which all our power lies. This is not to say that thought isn't useful. Thinking is an excellent and necessary tool, but we need to use it and not let it use us.

One day, I took a walk around our neighborhood in Delray Beach and came across a new house that was being constructed. I stopped to watch for a minute or two. There were so many different tradespeople working on the house at the same time: carpenters, plumbers, stonemasons, electricians. I realized that all these disparate people were working from the same set of architectural plans and shared the same objective, yet they all used different tools to accomplish their various tasks.

I was struck by the coordination and precision with which the builders used their many tools to build the house. If they had not learned how to use these tools properly, or didn't have the right tools for the job, it would be impossible to build the house.

It occurred to me how comparable this was to life. We are all trying to build our spiritual house, but often we do so in a limited way because we don't use all the tools we are given. For example, we try to use thought when what's really called for is surrender, or we reach for anger and blame when what we really need is compassion and forgiveness. Many times we use the old habit of judgment instead of the higher tool of acceptance, or we react with disappointment instead of choosing gratitude. I realized I needed two things: the awareness to remember that these tools were available to me and the discipline to choose them. When I did so, it changed my entire experience of life.

A Lesson in Love and Observing

One Saturday, I was visiting Dani in Philadelphia on one of our many weekend get-togethers. We were having dinner in a busy restaurant when Dani began to tell me about a new love interest.

"Dad, this new person I'm seeing is so funny and so smart, and we have so much in common and have great conversations that go on for hours," she said, her voice bubbling with excitement.

I felt my own heart lifting. I loved seeing her joy in the potential of a new relationship. Dani had dated a few guys in high school, but most of those relationships were short-lived. It made me happy that she could rediscover her capacity to have a meaningful relationship while still going through the grief of Christopher's death. It occurred to me that this would be the first time I wouldn't have Chris to help me size this guy up and make sure he knew that he better treat Dani right. Chris was an athlete and could be intimidating. It always made Alie and me feel safe that Dani's high school boyfriends knew they better not mess with her, otherwise they would have to answer to him.

Dani took a sip of her iced coffee before continuing her story. She glanced at the table, then met my eyes and said,

"And Dad. This person is a girl."

As my brain registered this unexpected announcement, my heart skipped a beat. This was years before there was openness to inclusion and certainly long before same-sex marriage was legal in the US. Outside of some big cities, there was a lot of closed-mindedness and even hate directed at the LGBTQ community. I wasn't sure how to respond and had many waves of emotions rising up inside of me within fractions of a second. I thought, *This could make her life more complicated, dealing with discrimination, or maybe even put her in danger? She always dated boys before. There were no hints or clues. Maybe this is a phase, or did Dani just come out to me?*

I wanted to be sure to say something supportive, so I just observed all these thoughts swarming inside my head but would not allow these waves to control my response. My practice of observing was critical that evening and allowed me to respond from a place of "What would love do now?"

I took a deep breath. With love and acceptance, I said, "Wow, Dani. I'm surprised and am so glad that you are comfortable enough to share this with me." We spent the rest of our dinner together chatting about her new girlfriend and how much I looked forward to meeting her.

On my drive home to New Jersey that night, I called Alie and told her about the conversation I'd just had with Dani. She, too, was completely taken by surprise. She thought that Dani might be going through a phase prompted by the death of her brother. Alie and I struggled with this new reality over the next few months as we both got caught in our old thoughts and patterns. We didn't always find the right words to convey our love and support to Dani. Even though that first evening went well, I realized that changing old beliefs and patterns required me to consistently choose new tools over and over. I feel so fortunate that, ultimately, the love in our family prevailed.

I will always be grateful that Dani felt secure enough to express her truth to me that day. The spiritual work we were all doing was helping us in all aspects of our lives. We all had Christopher to thank for that. We had found a way to continue to support Chris in his journey; we would certainly always support Dani in hers. All these years later, I am so thankful to have my daughter and her wife, my beautiful daughter-in-law, in our growing and close family.

From Observing to Transcendence

My interest in and obsession with the aspects of mind that lie *beyond* the layers of thought was growing. I found myself more and more attracted to finding quiet time in which I could explore this powerful dimension. My objective was not to suppress my thoughts but to let them flow without engaging them and to do this from my quiet space of observing. I would keep an open and curious mindset during these times and would find myself in a state of clarity. I wanted to know how to be in this space much more often.

Over the course of my reading, I was so intrigued by the many stories of people who reported that they had transcended thought and felt a complete sense of peace during a time of crisis in which they acted to help another person without thinking: For example, a woman who didn't know how to swim rescued a drowning child from the ocean, or a neighbor who ran into a burning house to retrieve an elderly man, and so many other acts of pure kindness, courage, and love.

During these moments of crisis, thinking shuts down, and the higher self takes over spontaneously. This is why these people never refer to themselves as heroes. They speak of the immense clarity they felt as they jumped into action without considering their own safety. They were not driven by thought, but by pure love to help someone in distress.

In other books and articles, I read stories about people who participated in extreme activities like skydiving and reported feeling a sense of calmness beyond thought. Athletes also speak about being in the "zone," where the outside world slows down and they have complete clarity and total focus on what they are doing without thinking about it. The thinking mind seems to let go when either exposed to situations that shock us out of our ordinary ways of experiencing life or in an activity that requires total and complete focus. Of most interest to me, however, were spiritual authors who discussed how they experienced a complete shutdown of thought and lived their life entirely in the Now. This was something I yearned to experience.

I'd had a brief glimpse of this state during the "rock bottom" moment in which my father held me as I cried, not long after Christopher's death. In that moment, my shock, sorrow, and grief were so intense they overwhelmed my thinking mind, and another door seemed to open. That experience had changed my life forever. I now realized I could keep this door open in my day-to-day life and practiced doing so often.

When I met with someone one-on-one, I practiced relaxing back into my quiet space of "no thought" and being fully present. This felt like a state of transcendence in which I was guided with words to say instead of thinking about my response. There were many times when I surprised myself with what I said, because I expressed ideas I'd never thought of before. My words would come across with such a strength and quality of empathy that it felt like we were both sharing a space of love together. This higher level of consciousness lies beyond thought.

Finding Direction

One of the places in which I searched for clues about how to open this door was in the research of Dr. David R. Hawkins, a psychiatrist and spiritual teacher who created the widely acclaimed Map of Consciousness. Hawkins created a scale that measures levels of consciousness from 0 to 1,000. Emotions like fear, worry, guilt, and pride are at low levels of energy or consciousness and register well under 200, which is the first level of integrity. States like love, peace, and compassion are at the highest levels and calibrate at 500 to 1,000, which is the highest level of consciousness of which humans are capable. According to Hawkins, states of acceptance and surrender bring us toward the most powerful energy accessible to humans.

I realized that the moments in which I "let go" and simply opened myself to guidance were the moments in which I accessed those higher levels of consciousness. When I let go, new ways of looking at these challenges would appear. I felt more clarity about the issue at hand than when I tried to think about what I was experiencing. This new dimension of "being" rather than thinking gave me a sense of conviction and confidence that my thoughts, opinions, and beliefs did not.

As I went about my work and home life, I began to be more sensitive and aware of where my mind was dwelling. Was I in low energy states, centered on only my needs and wants? Was I feeling sorry for myself, irritable toward others, or being a victim? Or was I coming from a place of expanded consciousness that included compassion, acceptance, and real love for others?

The more I observed my state of consciousness, the more I began to feel that I could choose that peaceful space in which my inner guidance was easier to hear and recognize. I likened this place to that much sought-after and spoken about "peace that surpasses all understanding." I wasn't staying in this space for very long periods at the time, but I knew that I could access it when I was journaling, meditating, or enjoying the quiet of my mind.

Letting Go of Thought

As I practiced living more of my life from this space of awareness above thought, I began to see the enormous amount of "programming" that I had bought into throughout my life. When I observed the blockages formed by old beliefs in my mind, I found that I no longer had to react to them. It felt like I was shaking off a cast that had been restricting me without my even realizing it.

Hawkins taught that thoughts are relative instead of absolute, and therefore, by definition, they cannot be based in truth. He said that because thinking is relative, it always includes both polarities. We argue for our side of the polarity; we have our opinions, judgments, and beliefs; and they appear to make us who we are. They seem to become our identity even though none of them are absolute reality. As I studied his work, I began to ask myself, who would I be without these concepts that I hold so dearly? Who would I be if I did not defend my judgments and opinions? I was becoming aware of a more quiet space in my mind that seemed above the thoughts, where I could retreat to and observe rather then react.

I was beginning to understand that the flow of life has nothing to do with my personal wants or preferences, but everything to do with my spiritual learning and awakening. Working with the Map of Consciousness helped me know that I had the potential to eventually express *only* love.

I was so grateful for these new understandings that had been initiated by Christopher's death. Losing my son had been a tragedy—but I could also see it as an opening, gifting me with a spiritual partnership that had transformed my way of experiencing life. Did I even need to label the experience of Christopher's death as a tragedy or an opening—or could I let our experience guide me toward a new awareness where I could rest in gratitude and love?

I had a feeling the answer to this question was "yes"—but my commitment to these ideas was about to be tested in a major way.

Chapter 7

The Power of Context Versus Content

Hi my wonderful son Chris,

There are so many times when I wish you were still here in human form. I could get your direct input on things, give you hugs, and we could celebrate so many milestones of life together. You would be so successful, and I would get to experience the pride of having such an amazing son. But life has given us this journey, and I accept.

I am working on being a humble and grateful part of life. This is God's world, and all is well in His world. I may not understand or agree, but that means very little, if anything. My responsibility is to accept, be grateful, move forward, and become an enlightened being. That is where I will have more understanding, and my questions can be answered. If you are closer to that, please help me understand. I love you and miss you.

Love forever and eternity,
Dad

ALIE AND I WERE having coffee together one morning when the doorbell rang. Alie went to answer the door, then came back into the kitchen holding a large, brown, official-looking envelope. She looked at me with a bit of apprehension and said, "Steve, this is from Detective Walsh." Detective Brian Walsh was a man in his late thirties, married with two children. He loved his job and was excellent at it. He and I and our family had grown close over the course of the investigation of Chris's accident. In the course of our conversations we would often discuss family. Detective Walsh shared with me that his own brother had died in an accident. He told me he could fully understand what we were going through. I felt grateful to have such a compassionate man in law enforcement to be working with us. Now, all that investigative work was complete, and we knew what this envelope would have in it.

With shaky hands, Alie opened the thick envelope. As expected, it was the final report on Christopher's accident. Just seeing the cover page with all its official stamps and markings sent a flood of emotions through me. I even felt a bit queasy as I was taken back to that life-changing morning, standing in that bright hospital room, with the nurse and police officer standing respectfully nearby.

So much had changed since that day. We had all been through rough and difficult times of grief and were just beginning to experience tiny glimmers of healing. Seeing the police report felt like being pulled back in time to those chaotic early days of disbelief, anger, despair, and the unimaginable sadness that just seemed to loop over and over in my mind. My heart beat a little harder, and my palms began to sweat as the physical intensity of those moments came back to me.

Alie began to read the report to herself, her eyes scanning the pages quickly as she searched for any new information that might shed light on Christopher's death. Although Alie knew very well that nothing in that document would bring back our son, I also understood that she wanted to know every detail in a way that I just didn't. When it comes to grief, everybody's journey is different. Alie and I each had to follow our own path; luckily, we had always made room for those differences and never put pressure on ourselves to grieve in the same way.

As Alie read each page of the report in silence and in tears, I made the decision, right there and then, that I was not going to read the summary of that fateful evening. I knew it could only take me down paths of blame, sadness, and spinning stories of what could have been or should have been done. I did not want to be tempted into this mental activity, as I had been finding more peace and clarity by making more deliberate choices. I had already accepted the fact that Chris's journey was designed to be twenty-three years, and I did not want to move backward when my inner path was calling me forward. I supported Alie's decision to read the report, but I knew this choice was not for me.

Content Versus Context

Later that day, as I was taking some quiet time to journal and meditate, I recalled the concept of content and context that Dr. David Hawkins often wrote about. Hawkins defined *content* as the circumstances, the situation at hand, or the more apparent and literal matter being dealt with. *Context* is a much larger perspective that includes deeper meaning and significance.

I recognized that I could get caught up in content when my attention was engaged only on the surface of an experience, or when I did not stay present in my interactions with people. I would get caught up in complaining, opinions, and even judgments when in this narrow mindset, and these reactions could feel like "who I am." However, when I stepped back and looked at the *context*, I could be interested and curious instead of judgmental and reactive.

For example, when I got frustrated because my flight from New Jersey to Florida was delayed, it was easy to complain about the airlines and the lines at the airport, which is the *content* of the circumstance at hand. But when I shifted my focus to the *context*, I could feel gratitude for this amazing time we live in where I can have the lifestyle of living and working in two states that are fifteen hundred miles from each other.

I would remind myself of how fortunate I am that our airline industry is so safe and flies me through the sky at six hundred miles per hour to get me back home in time for dinner most Friday evenings. Choosing to focus on this expanded context put me in a much calmer and more accepting mindset.

Dr. Hawkins taught that we deal with the *content* of our life experiences every moment of the day, and if we have the awareness to see the higher *context* of our experiences, we gain access to a wider range of choices in how to respond. To me, these ideas very much related to the police report Alie and I had received earlier that day. While I fully understood that this report might help with some level of closure, it would only be closure to the *content*. It would not provide me the deeper answers that could only come from the *context*. Content can be so compelling to our thought-based mind that we become completely wrapped up in it, but my choice was to seek peace and choose another way.

I found this new awareness to be life-changing. For example, when I was speaking to Alie or with our daughters, I was able to truly listen and hear what they were expressing, even if I may not agree with the content at times. I was listening to them to truly understand and not just to respond. In business meetings, too, I found that I could help everyone move forward by viewing issues from a larger context. Many times, people get caught up in what I refer to as "admiring the problem"—in other words, getting pulled deeper and deeper into the content. But when we reconnect to the bigger context, the very problem we've been admiring often has a way of resolving itself.

Switching from content to context felt like a superpower. It allowed me to shift my mental energy away from a narrow view filled with thinking and instead slow down, relax into the situation, and quiet my mind. This opened me up to more compassionate responses that were only possible from this higher vantage point. I knew this was one more way in which the experience of Christopher's death was teaching me so much more about life.

Learning from the Universe

Getting the police report in the mail was a milestone moment in which I realized how far this journey had taken me already. I recognized how often I had previously been so caught up in the content of life that I'd sometimes failed to appreciate life's beauty and mystery. Now, I took great comfort in letting my mind soar on little trips that always seemed to take me deeper into that mystery. I would sit outside in the evening and stare at the sky, letting myself be dazzled by the stars, or let my mind roam free when I went for long runs, looking up at the beautiful blue dome above me and feeling life flowing through me without thinking.

My mind could also soar on these trips when I read books about astronomy by authors like Carl Sagan, Neil deGrasse Tyson, and astronaut Edgar Mitchell. These amazing authors teach that we live on a small blue planet that is rocketing through an expanding space, spinning around, and circling in a solar system somewhere in a galaxy contained in a vast universe. Science has proven that there are hundreds of millions of stars like our sun, and that's just in our own Milky Way galaxy. There are hundreds of millions of galaxies in our incomprehensible universe, and we have no real idea where we are in this universe or where we are going.

When I was at our home in Delray Beach, I would gaze at the beautiful, clear Florida night sky over the ocean, and it would open my mind and give me a sense of reverence and awe for this mystery of which we are all a part. I found it so compelling to read about the number of scientific discoveries being made of new stars and planets as well as galaxies and the mysterious black holes that are hundreds of millions of light-years away. I was amazed to learn that we can detect light that left its source almost at the time of the big bang, fourteen billion years ago.

These mind-expanding trips always inspired me and made me feel humbled. When I contemplated the universe, it was so easy to see that life was incomprehensibly vast, mysterious, and complex, and that we humans are only beginning to understand it. I would reflect on the profound insight I learned from Eckhart Tolle that "for the first time on this planet, consciousness is becoming aware of itself through each of us." I realized that I could see myself as insignificant in the content of life, or I could see myself as an integral expression and awareness of all this amazing life flowing through me.

It seems obvious, but it is interesting to acknowledge that all we know, and the entire history of humanity, has all occurred on this tiny blue planet. We've come so far in our understanding of astronomy, when it was only a couple hundred years ago that most humans believed the earth was flat and that the earth was the center of the universe. If we could be so wrong about those things for such a long time, what else are we missing and have yet to discover?

Far from making me despair, contemplating humanity's unknowingness only deepened my sense of awe. What new discoveries in scientific and quantum science research, as well as consciousness research, were still to come within my lifetime? Surely, some of them would shed light on the mysteries of death, and on the questions that had guided my life ever since Christopher's passing.

When I journaled with Chris, I would find myself asking questions like, *Who am I really? What am I?* and *What is the purpose of it all?* I experienced a deepening understanding of these age-old questions when I quieted my mind and approached them from a place of stillness.

Contemplating the universe became an important exercise in my healing. I could see that all life is happening perfectly and must have a purpose—and that everything from the shape of a spiral galaxy to the trajectory of a human life is beautiful if I could see it from this larger perspective. Even though I don't always understand and may not agree with life and the circumstances it gives me, I can accept that the highest purpose of life is for me to awaken to my spiritual essence. I can accept that every experience I have at any given time is for the sole purpose of my growth. I can accept that life is good, and I can always find my happiness and peace within no matter what is going on outside. My only other choice is to resist the flow of life, to fight with life, and basically tell life that my plan is better than life's plan. It's futile to try to change the shape of the galaxy—so why should I try to change the shape of life?

An Important Anniversary

The one-year anniversary of Chris's death was approaching. I could hardly believe all that had changed during that time. Just twelve months ago, we'd been living in Colt's Neck, New Jersey, surrounded by horse pastures, maple trees, and beautiful neighborhoods spread out on acres of property. Christopher was making a name for himself at the firm, and I felt so excited to talk to him every day and to celebrate every milestone on his path of mastering the business. Our family life was a happy swirl of watching our children grow into their lives, enjoying the warmth and love of family gatherings, and working through the ups and downs that occured, and I assumed the future would look exactly as I'd imagined it, with Christopher, Dani, and Alex growing up, getting married, and having kids of their own.

Afterward, my whole understanding of life and death was turned upside down, and every aspect of my existence underwent a profound change. Alie, Alex, and I were living in a new house in a different state. Dani was in culinary school in Philadelphia, and Alex was going to a new school. My work life was different now that I was commuting, and my orientation in life shifted fully toward the spiritual. The material world was becoming much less important to me, and I was seeing life through new eyes.

My relationships, too, changed tremendously. Whereas many couples are torn apart after the death of a child, Alie and I grew closer, realizing we were the only two people who had this exact experience of Chris's death and who played a crucial role in supporting our daughters as they moved forward. Even though Alie and I had different styles of grieving, we made space for each other to do things in our own way. We encouraged each other to seek support from friends and family members instead of trying to meet each other's every need. Our marriage was stronger than ever, and we both felt that Christopher was guiding our family to be closer in every way.

I'd always had a wide social circle of business associates, golf buddies, and fellow parents, but I now found that I gravitated toward people with whom I could have deeper and more meaningful conversations. Conversations about travel or the last vacation were fine, but I found they were not as interesting as they used to be. I wanted to surround myself with people who were seeking to evolve their consciousness and follow their inner pathway, just as I was learning to follow mine. I found these connections with some family members and friends, as well as in my *A Course in Miracles* class and other spiritual study groups.

In our family, it was a tradition to have a joint birthday party for Alex and Christopher, since their birthdays were just a few days apart. Often, we'd celebrate my father Al's birthday, which was also in December, making for a triple birthday party. As the one-year anniversary of Christopher's death approached, which was also his birthday, Alie and I grappled with the question of how to make Alex's ninth birthday a happy one, even as we acknowledged the anniversary of Christopher's death.

We decided to spend Alex's birthday and the Christmas holidays at our condo in New Jersey, where we would be close to extended family and friends. Tieal would fly up from Florida to be with us, and Dani would drive in from Philadelphia. We would put both Alex and Christopher's names on the cake, just like we always had, and send our love to both of them when Alex blew the candles out.

After spending so much time at the condo alone, it was amazing to have Alie, Alex, Dani, and Tieal there with me. The quiet rooms I'd used for journaling and meditation were filled with the sounds of people talking, cooking, wrapping presents, decorating the Christmas tree, and watching movies. Dani had recently adopted two rescue kittens, and we were all so entertained by watching them explore and even climb the Christmas tree, knocking down ornaments on the way. It was a joy to set aside my quiet lifestyle in that condo for a couple of weeks and thoroughly embrace the loving presence of my family.

I felt grateful that Tieal had remained so close to our family after Christopher died. She brought another dimension of Chris's life to us, but Alie and I worried about her. In a letter she sent me shortly after her graduation from college, she'd written, *I am still grieving for sure and I still wonder why this has happened to all of us. I do blame myself for a lot of that night because I should have been in New Jersey for his birthday, and if I had been then this all would have been different. I feel a lot of guilt for the situation and I have not really explained that to you all. I feel like I could have changed the situation if I had just picked up the phone when he called and I can't sleep at night because I just keep replaying that night over and over in my head.*

Even though there was nothing Tieal could have done to prevent Christopher's death, she was haunted by the sense that if she'd "only" taken time off work, or picked up the phone during her shift at work, she could have altered the course of life. Watching Tieal wrestle with these thoughts was a stark reminder of the critical importance of acceptance in the grieving process. I respected the fact that Tieal's journey was unique, but I wished I could help her see that thinking you could have changed the circumstances and content of life is a losing battle. No matter how much we tried to reassure her, she felt that it was all her fault. As I watched her mental health suffering, I hoped that I could say or do something that would help her before it was too late.

Life Is Happening by Me

On the day that we celebrated Alex and Christopher's birthdays, our condo was filled with relatives and close friends. I remembered the way our old house had flooded with people in the days and weeks after Christopher died and how their physical presence was such a source of comfort. I felt that same kind of love on this day. Everyone went out of their way to make Alex feel special, asking her questions about her new school in Florida and about the many swim competitions she was doing. And when Alex was out of earshot, different family members came up to Alie and me to remark on how well she was doing, one short year after the trauma.

The birthday cake was big enough to feed an army and had the words *Happy Birthday Alex and Christopher* beautifully written in icing. When we lit the candles, I felt Christopher's presence strongly and knew that he would be so proud to watch his little sister growing up into such a wonderful young lady. Just as I felt gratitude to have a spiritual partner on the "other side," I felt grateful that Alex had Christopher watching over her—although of course I would have preferred if he was standing beside her, helping blow out the candles on their shared cake.

After the party wound down, I went into my writing room for some quiet time. Sitting in contemplation, I remembered a profound insight I'd once heard from a spiritual teacher: "Life is not happening to me but is happening by me." This short but powerful phrase expressed clearly that I have the power to choose how I want to experience the events of my life. I do not control life and its unfolding, but I do control my response, and this is how life "happens by me."

Christopher's death hadn't happened *to* me; neither had any of the events in my life. Instead, they were simply *happening*, and I was choosing how I would experience my life through my response. When I look at life this way, I remember that my choices are what create my reality. I am never a victim to anyone or anything. This simple fact empowers me and enables me to experience life in the way I choose.

I would need all of this understanding and strength when Tieal hit her own rock-bottom moment just a few months later.

Chapter 8

The Miracle of Choosing Another Way

Hey Chris,

I feel that I continue to move ahead toward my spiritual reality—the only thing that is important and necessary for this life. Love is the key and starts with love of self, Mom, Dani, Alex, and you. I also feel that the hold of my thought-based mind is weakening slowly. It is scary because of the perceived loss of control—but if I control nothing in the larger world of context, then I control nothing in the smaller world of content of mind and human stuff.

I am learning to allow the flow of life through me and to surrender each moment to God. I have faith in the Universal plan of which I am a part. That is the only Reality and I get to observe it thanks to the level of consciousness expressing itself through me. Our relationship has allowed me to understand my spiritual self. Thank You.

Love forever and eternity,
Dad

IN THE WEEKS AFTER Christmas, Tieal and I had long conversations about the blame she placed on herself for Christopher's death. She told me that Chris had wanted her to take the trip from Florida to New Jersey with him, but she'd decided to stay in Boca Raton and squeeze in a couple more days of work before the holidays. After all, Chris would be spending Christmas with her family in New Orleans, so they would only be apart for a few days.

"Mr. Ferrara, if I'd been in New Jersey, Christopher wouldn't have even gone out that night," Tieal would say. "We would have stayed home with you all, and none of this would have happened."

She would begin to cry as she recalled the missed calls from him on her cell phone. "I wasn't allowed to answer my phone at work—I didn't even have it on me—but if I'd just seen those calls in time, I could have stepped out and at least talked to him."

Tieal blamed herself mercilessly. At the same time, she would tell me about the impact Christopher had had on her life, showing her what it felt like to be truly loved. How could she go on after losing the love of her life? How could she step into a future where he wasn't there to love and encourage her every day?

Just like Alie, Dani, Alex, and me, Tieal sometimes got "signs" from Chris in the form of dreams or coincidences. One night, her friends took her to a Maroon 5 concert to try to cheer her up. Maroon 5 was Chris and Tieal's favorite band, and Chris's favorite song, as I mentioned, was "She Will Be Loved," which he sang to her often while driving together in the car. At about the midpoint of the concert, when Tieal was already feeling Chris's presence strongly, Maroon 5 went on to play a beautiful version of "She Will Be Loved." At the end of the song, the lead singer, Adam Levine, shouted into the microphone in front of ten thousand people, "That was for Tieal!" Needless to say, Tieal was stunned, and while she knew there must have been another Tieal he was referring to, it felt like Christopher was speaking directly to her. When she told me about this, I was speechless. It filled me with a feeling of warmth, excitement, and gratitude to know that our ongoing connection with Chris was undeniable. He seemed to be there at the exact times we needed him.

But still, Tieal yearned to be close to Chris and to somehow go back in time and alter reality so that his death would not have taken place. She was sleepless night after night and tormented herself with thoughts that she and she alone could have prevented his death. Then one day, Tieal hit rock bottom. Her mother called me to say that she had attempted suicide, and they had rushed her to the hospital. I immediately felt a gripping fear and sadness throughout my body. I could feel my energy just draining out and could almost fall over from the weakness in my legs. It was all I could do to eke out the words, "How is she?" I couldn't even imagine how our families could bear the pain of losing Tieal, as we were still only taking small steps forward after Chris's tragic death.

Tieal's mother Laura told me that they had gotten help in time, and thankfully Tieal was in stable condition and wanted to speak with me. When Tieal's mother put her on the phone, she was crying so hard she could barely speak. "I'm sorry, Mr. Ferrara," she said. "I don't want to cause anyone any pain. I just couldn't see a way forward without Christopher."

I was so relieved and happy to hear her voice and felt a strong wave of gratitude at knowing that she was okay. Hearing that pain in her voice brought me back to my own rock-bottom moment. I remembered that while this moment felt like the end, it was actually the beginning of my healing. I hoped that this could be hers.

At some point in our lives, we get to a place deep within where we realize that there must be a better way. This is a critical point where real and sustained change has the potential to be made. It often seems to come at a moment of intense grief, pain, sadness, or desperation, where all of our thought-based tools and rationalizations become meaningless, and we have no choice but to surrender.

I could easily recall what it felt like to be in such mental and physical pain, to feel hopeless with no answers, to feel like this misery was permanent, there was no way out of it, it would never end. And I remembered the exact moment when my mind seemed to let go, and I got a small glimpse into another perspective—a tiny opening of light and understanding making itself known to me.

I felt that Tieal was having her own breakthrough as she cried uncontrollably. Her pain brought her to the brink of almost losing her life, and now that pain would lead her to choosing another way where she could allow this experience to be a teacher and guide.

From Blame to Acceptance

In our many conversations after her suicide attempt, I continued to reassure Tieal that her only mistake was placing the blame for Christopher's death on herself—she had done nothing wrong and could not have changed the course of Christopher's destiny in any way. Life unfolds perfectly; we each have our journey, and we always have a choice as to how we will respond to the challenges that life throws at us. I shared with her the times when I also went down the path of blame: times when I would have angry thoughts that the universe had screwed up and this was not supposed to happen, or Chris's death could have and should have been avoided. I told her that in my darkest moments, I put the blame on everyone and everything, including God.

I distinctly remember shortly after Chris died that there was a terrible tsunami in the Indian Ocean that struck Indonesia. It killed over 200,000 people and caused unbearable suffering in that part of the world. Alie immediately felt that this terrible event and Chris's death by drowning were related. Nature was making mistakes, and none of this should be happening. We were both in such grief and anguish at that point, stuck in our thoughts, and lashing out at anything and everything. The universe, or even God, had to be wrong because it made no sense to wipe out 200,000 people or to take our perfect and beautiful son.

I also went through a period when blaming myself seemed to make sense. The accident happened on Chris's birthday, and there were so many alternate scenarios that ran through my mind. I would run through all the could-haves and would-haves and especially should-haves. I could have gotten him a car service to take him and his friends to Atlantic City, which was where they originally wanted to go. We could have done something together at home to celebrate his birthday that evening. I should have spent more time with him before he left with his friends, which was the last time I would see him alive and have been able to give him a hug.

All these thoughts carried tremendous sadness and heavy negative and painful feelings. They pulled me in, and I even felt a strange satisfaction from beating myself up during this period. I told Tieal that it was only by accepting the *flow of life,* by respecting the power and perfection of the Universe, and by letting go of wanting life to conform to my needs and wants, that I found a bigger purpose for the tragedy of losing Chris. Focusing on my love for Chris and supporting his life journey, whether I agreed with it or not, enabled me to move forward and embrace the potential of this otherwise unimaginably painful time. I shared this conviction with Tieal often when we spoke on the phone and when we met for our many lunches in Delray, and she began to open to this mindset adjustment within herself.

Over the following months and years, our family stayed close to Tieal. I watched as she grew from this rock-bottom time in her life to find a healthy and loving way to move forward. She truly went from unbearable grief to acceptance to gratitude that Chris was on his journey. She accepted that this was his destiny and there was nothing she could have done to change that. She still felt sadness, but her love for Chris enabled her to support his ongoing journey while staying committed to moving forward in hers.

It took quite a while, but she eventually dated again, and I could not be more grateful that she is now happily married with two beautiful daughters. Alie and I even got to see how it felt to be grandparents when Tieal visited us with her children. Her husband is fully aware of the love that she has for Chris and supports her in her ongoing journey and relationship with him.

Learning from Guilt and Blame

Long after Christopher's death, I was struck by the prevalence of guilt as an aspect of the grieving process. In my journaling with Chris, I began to write about the nature of guilt. In my inner observations, I recognized how guilt was an underlying feeling that I often carried for no apparent reason. It was a heavy burden of suffering that I sometimes *thought* I needed to feel—as if it was my duty or a debt I owed. But when I stopped to question this guilt, I realized it had no real purpose. My feeling guilty didn't right some wrong in the world, and it certainly didn't alleviate anyone's suffering. Yet it still felt like guilt was the "correct" emotion to have and that people made a peculiar bond with each other by expressing feelings of guilt.

Guilt is a socially acceptable response in our culture that we all recognize and understand. When a person dies, it can seem like feeling guilty is the right way to feel, especially if that person's death was unexpected. *We could have done more, I could have been there for them more*, or even, *Why am I still here when they are not?* Expressing guilt, and its companion, blame, will attract sympathy and sorrow from others. It is a pattern we can play out again and again, but in the long run it offers no relief and only prolongs our suffering.

In addition, guilt has been used for millennia as a controlling tool by religion, our parents, teachers, and almost all in authority to keep us in check. As a child, I was brought up in a religion that taught that I should feel deep guilt if I did something wrong. If I felt guilty enough, then maybe God would be easier on me and not punish me so severely for my sin.

As an adult, these old habit patterns of blame and guilt played themselves out in a "knee-jerk" reactionary way, and it seemed like this was the way it was supposed to be. These concepts and beliefs are buried deep within. It takes vigilant observation and commitment to become aware of them and ultimately let them go. I recognized that guilt was a corrosive emotion, with no purpose or function, and lead to toxic feelings that could destroy me from the inside out. I needed to focus on healing, knowing that I was allowed to be joyful even though my son had died. Ultimately, gratitude for life and acceptance for the way it flowed is crucial, as opposed to resisting it and feeling fear, blame, and guilt.

With these thoughts in mind, I came up with a process for getting out of the recurring trap that guilt and blame create and *finding another way* to view these experiences. This simple but not easy process helped me catch myself before I went too far down the road of suffering or despair from guilt, blame, and judgment. I started from the important premise that we are all flawed human beings prone to making correctable mistakes, as opposed to punishable sins or irreversible faults. Far from being opportunities for condemnation of ourselves or others, the mistakes we make contain the ingredients for learning.

This realization allowed me to approach my mistakes and the mistakes of others with a more compassionate and forgiving mindset. The healthy and responsible attitude of a correctable and forgivable mistake changed everything, as it included the transformative power of both forgiveness and love.

The three-step process to *choose to find another way* goes like this:

1. *Start by viewing our responses of blame, guilt, or judgment of ourselves or others as a correctable mistake.*

   This first step puts us back in a position of responsibility with the power to correct, learn from, and choose another way.

2. *Use the higher tool of forgiveness by forgiving ourselves and others for reacting with blame, guilt, or judgment.*

   This allows us to move from condemnation to compassion.

3. *Choose a better way by simply asking, What would love do now?*

   This creates a safety net of compassion and understanding that catches us before we spiral too far into negativity.

Adopting a Student Mindset

I was beginning to accept that this human experience has only one real purpose in the grandest context: to learn from and be awakened by our life experiences. We are students in a classroom during our time on earth. If I keep an open and curious attitude, I can learn from every experience in my life, freed from the pressure of needing to have all the answers. I realized that the greatest lessons are inherent in the most challenging experiences. While the feeling passing through may be uncomfortable and even painful at times, I know that it won't kill me and I can look at these experiences as opportunities for growth.

The truth is, we are all on our individual journeys. We are *all* spiritual beings having this human experience, and we are all doing the best we can with what we have. My timeline will look different from anyone else's. Nobody is "ahead," and nobody is "behind;" we are all learning the right thing at exactly the right time. When I think about life in this way, I see how we truly are all in our own curriculum. I become more accepting and less judgmental, and I can feel love and compassion for people and life more easily.

Gratitude Is a Window to the Soul

Among the many sorrows I felt about Christopher's passing, I felt a tremendous sense of loss over not getting to work with him and watch him rise through the ranks at the company. During the months since he'd joined the firm, Chris and I had really enjoyed working together. We would go to client meetings and play off each other's energy, practically finishing one another's sentences. Clients always responded so well to seeing the next generation entering the business and would be impressed by Chris's ideas and professionalism. I missed the joy and bonding I felt during the one-on-one time we had driving to appointments together, discussing his progress and answering the many questions he had about our profession. Many times, I felt a sense of deep sadness and loneliness when I was at work because I missed him so much.

As I journaled with Chris about this loneliness, I began to feel a shift in my mindset away from the sadness of missing him and toward a feeling of gratitude for the ongoing relationship that he and I still shared. I started a habit of always carrying a picture of Chris with me in my shirt pocket, close to my heart. If I felt sadness when I saw other fathers and sons interacting in business or on a golf course, or I saw other young advisors who reminded me of Chris, I would look at the picture of my son. It would remind me that I could choose another way to have this experience. This other way was to have gratitude for the window to my soul that our relationship opened and for all that we were learning together. Gratitude was becoming a great healer.

When I had been practicing this for some time, I realized that I could have experiences similar to the ones I had with Chris by working more closely with some of our other young advisors who were his peers and friends in our firm. Although Christopher would never walk into the office again, I could build strong connections with these young people who would have been his colleagues; I would feel more fulfilled and Chris's spirit could live on through them.

I began working with many of the young associates, coaching and mentoring and sharing my experience with them. One of the young advisors I took under my wing was Chris's best friend, Justin, who had joined our firm on the same day as Chris and had been there on the night of his death. I'd known Justin since he was thirteen years old, when he and Christopher met on their first day of high school. They quickly became inseparable, working out and playing together, spending time at our home or Justin's, and always having each other's backs in the many adventures they had together. If Christopher had lived, I knew that Justin would have been best man at his wedding and an uncle or godfather to his kids, and vice versa.

During our coaching sessions, Justin would share stories of Chris with me—the kinds of things that could only be experienced with a best friend. We would laugh and cry and thoroughly enjoy each session and look forward to the next. I coached Justin in the science and art of the business, and he showed just as much energy and ambition to learn as Christopher had.

Justin and Chris took a cross-country road trip together after college, right before joining me in business, during which they made friends everywhere and had so many life-changing experiences. Justin told me about the time they visited the Grand Canyon on one of the hottest days of the year. The rangers were warning people to take short hikes and not even attempt to hike down the canyon. It was 115 degrees when they arrived, and Chris was dealing with a sprained ankle from a run the day before. Nevertheless, Christopher and Justin decided that they were in great shape compared to the rangers and they could do it together.

Justin told me that Chris said, "All these people are older and out of shape, and *we* can do this!" They proceeded down the canyon with a gallon of water and some peanut butter protein bars. They not only made it down the canyon but also hiked back up, making the treacherous twelve-plus-mile round-trip hike in about twelve hours.

Justin told me, "There were times when we didn't think we would make it back up, but we just kept pushing each other. Neither one of us could have done this alone, but the bond of our friendship and support for each other got us to dig deeper and find every bit of strength we needed to get back to the top."

It gave me such joy to hear these stories and learn about sides of Chris that I would not have known about otherwise. His passion and love for life and the inspiration he provided to others made me realize that he had really *lived* a full life during his time on earth—that he had known love, adventure, and friendship at a level that many people may not find in a lifetime.

Justin and I still meet once a month after all these years. We've formed a lifelong bond, and I've had the privilege of being part of his life as he's grown into being a great husband and father and highly successful advisor. He used the Grand Canyon experience as motivation to develop into an ultimate runner, consistently running one-hundred-mile marathons where he says he still feels the presence of Christopher by his side during the toughest times.

Another young advisor I worked with closely was my nephew Joey, Christopher's younger cousin by seven years. Joey always reminded me so much of Chris in looks and personality. I was thrilled when he joined our firm and immediately took him under my wing. The closeness I felt with Joey was very similar to the closeness I felt with Chris, and this filled me with so much gratitude. It made me wonder if Joey joining our firm might have been a Christopher intervention.

During our coaching times together, Joey would share stories with me from when Chris and he were kids. Chris was an excellent athlete in soccer and basketball, and he would take the time to teach Joey how to excel in those sports. Joey told me how Chris and he would spend hours on our driveway basketball court, Chris teaching him how to shoot, dribble, and play defense. These coaching sessions started when Joey was only five years old and Chris was twelve. Despite Joey's young age, Chris would continually encourage him to work hard. Joey said, "He would tell me I was going to be as good as Michael Jordan and that I could be great at anything I chose to do in life."

The bonds I created with so many of our young advisors exist even today. I feel so fortunate to experience in many ways what I would have experienced with Chris. Choosing to find another way was a miracle that changed my life experience from the sadness of missing those times with Chris to the joy of mentoring our young advisors. And when I let go of my own ideas of how life "should" have been, Chris's legacy began to make itself known in ways I never could have predicted.

Chapter 9

Taking Full Responsibility

Hey Chris,

The human dimension of "me" can still feel sad or sorry for myself at times, but my spiritual reality, for which you are my window, helps me know we are together.

Humanness is very distracting, with endless physical and mental stimulation, but our relationship refocuses me when I am aware. There is nothing more important in my life than spiritual awareness, and you have given me and Mom and Dani and Alex the precious gift of a spiritual opening in our very human lives.

How blessed am I? Thank You.

Love forever and eternity,
Dad

AS I STEPPED FURTHER into the role of mentor and confidant for Tieal, Justin, Joey, and the many other young people who were close with Christopher in and out of our firm, I was amazed by the way our bonds of love with Chris made our relationships with each other so strong. By keeping an open and accepting mindset, and always remembering to ask myself, "What would love do now?" I found I could provide guidance and insights to these young people in ways that might not have been possible for me before. I felt I was becoming a more accepting and compassionate version of myself due to my consistent spiritual practice. I was learning to listen deeply and be fully present in all my relationships. The strong sense of Christopher's presence that I felt when I was around his friends let me know that he was still affecting their lives. We were all learning and growing together and felt that he was watching out for us just as he always had.

My relationship with my father had deepened even further in the time since Christopher's death. As my dad was getting older, he was a little slower and sometimes not as sharp as he had always been. Still, we would meet regularly for hours-long meals at diners in both New Jersey and Florida and have great discussions about life, love, and our experiences on the path to spiritual awakening.

Our conversations always included Chris. We both felt strongly that the three of us were somehow traveling together. In a strange way, it even felt like Chris was leading us. The three of us had always been so close, maybe even linked at the soul level for a very long time. We knew that our relationship with Chris had transcended his death.

I felt fortunate that Chris was with me and within me. I never had to call him, text him, email him, or find time to see him, as he was always "available" for me. I felt that I was taking full responsibility for the experience of Chris's death by choosing to have him remain part of my life in a healthy and joyful way. I realized that my dad and others who knew and loved Chris were having a similar experience, and that he continued to influence their lives just as he was influencing mine.

The Power of a Vision

Chris had spent his last day on earth planning his career goals for the upcoming year, with a clear focus on winning the coveted National New Advisor of the Year Award. Every year, over one thousand young advisors across the country compete for this award; it is the highest honor for a new advisor in our industry. Years before he joined the firm, Chris had already dreamed of winning this award. Our firm's top advisor, Jack, had been the last person from our company to win the award, twenty-five years prior. Over the years, he and Chris had developed a friendship. When Jack and his family would visit our home, he and Chris would spend hours on our basketball court talking about Chris's interest in our profession. Chris longed to follow in Jack's footsteps by joining the firm and bringing home the New Advisor award.

Huddled at his manager's desk on this fateful day, which was also his birthday, Chris laid out his objectives in minute detail: from the number of new clients he would need to develop, to the amount of new business he would need to produce, to the marketing plans he would implement. He had a clear vision with complete strategies, combined with a conviction to do all he had to do to win and bring this award back to our firm after twenty-five years.

At the end of his plan, Christopher added an important note: "If I do not win this award, someone from our firm needs to win. It has been way too long."

Chris's commitment was well known among our new associates. Now, after his tragic passing, Justin and Jack teamed up. It quickly became their mission and total focus to execute Chris's plan. Even before Chris had joined the company, Jack had been mentoring Chris and sharing his enormous experience and wisdom with him. Their bond had grown even tighter as Chris's career accelerated under Jack's tutelage. Justin would now benefit from Jack's generous leadership as they worked together to accomplish Chris's dream. Justin and Jack's unique and loving relationships with Chris took their commitment to Chris's vision to a level of resolute determination.

They worked tirelessly together week after week, propelled by a drive to keep Chris's dream alive. Jack became like a new advisor all over again, working very long hours side by side with Justin and going to his client meetings, with Jack sharing all his experience and coaching Justin each step of the way.

Whenever Justin doubted himself, Jack was there to assure him of his talents. They built a partnership based on their single-minded purpose to make Chris's dream a reality.

By year's end, Justin had produced an amount of new business almost equal to the exact objective to which Chris had committed in his plan, and Jack broke all national production records held for years by other veteran advisors around the country. Their determination and energy was palpable and literally carried our firm, creating a much-needed enthusiasm during an otherwise very tough first year after Christopher's death. They went on to win both the coveted National New Advisor of the Year Award and the National Senior Advisor Award, which had never been done by two advisors in the same firm during the same year.

We all attended the National Conference held in May of the following year and watched with enormous pride when both Justin and Jack were awarded these national distinctions. I imagined how honored Christopher would feel watching his best friend walking up to the stage and being recognized in this way and how they would celebrate together afterward, sharing the joy and excitement just as they always had.

Both Jack and Justin were asked to give an acceptance speech. In front of over one thousand people in the audience, they both spoke eloquently about Christopher, our family, and what we all meant to them.

"The person who inspired me to strive for this award was my best friend, Christopher Ferrara," Justin said. "We both joined the firm as advisors on the same day, and he was always pushing me to do my best. Whether we were calling new business owners or networking with people or visiting with a client, he would impress everyone with his passion and love for our profession. He had a personality and charm that attracted people of all ages and walks of life and made them feel happy. Chris was the person I could always count on. He always had my back, we were business partners, and he was another brother to me. I dedicate this great honor and award to him."

When it was Jack's turn to speak, he said, "Chris was a special person that you don't meet often in life. He was loving, he enjoyed life to the fullest, and he was joyful to be around. I was so energized and inspired by Chris's attitude and work ethic and so deeply touched by his care and compassion for people and love for our profession. I thank Chris and the Ferrara family for inspiring me and dedicate this award to them."

The level of enthusiasm and close family culture that has always existed in our firm grew immensely thanks to Justin and Jack's efforts, the lofty levels they attained, and the way they shared their affection for Chris and our organization so freely with all. After the ceremony, we all celebrated and hugged and had many laughs and cries as we all felt Chris's presence and knew that his vision to bring the New Advisor of the Year Award back to our firm was what had propelled these achievements.

But his vision did not stop there. Shortly after this national conference, I got a call from the CEO of Guardian, the financial services company that gives these awards. He told me he'd been moved by what Justin and Jack had said about Christopher.

"Steve," he said, "would you give me your permission to rename the National New Advisor of the Year Award in honor of Chris?"

I immediately felt a wave of gratitude, humility, and joy that this major corporation and this CEO took the time to consider something so heartfelt. I was honored beyond words. Guardian Life is a huge company, with thousands of employees spread out across the US and around the world. My own firm was just one of hundreds of financial firms and offices operating in the Guardian network with tens of thousands of advisors and brokers. It was beyond anything I could ever imagine to think of Christopher's memory being honored at every national convention and how this would enable his vision to live on.

All these years later, the Christopher Ferrara New Advisor of the Year award has gone on to inspire thousands of young advisors. Alie and I have had the great honor of awarding the winner each year and hearing each recipient speak with so much affection and respect about the inspiration they felt from Chris and his story. It was incredible to watch Chris's personal goal expand into a context far greater than he or anyone could have imagined.

I understood that when a vision is powered by conviction and love, it mysteriously aligns with the universe and can even transcend death. Chris's dream inspired Jack and Justin and ultimately an entire company. This award continues to be the most prestigious award given to a new advisor, and Chris's story has brought an even higher purpose and value to becoming a part of this community. Many recipients have shared with me that while receiving the award is wonderful, knowing the meaning and significance provides an inner fulfilment far beyond the outer accolades.

Chris's passion for our profession is forever memorialized, and I get to feel the joy of us "working together" in our third-generation firm, helping others reach their highest potential.

My Continued Search for Peace

The spiritual authors whose books I admired often pointed out that the thinking mind is always pulling from the past or future and is rarely in the present moment. Our experience of reality is therefore colored by old patterns and habits as well as layers of concepts, judgments, beliefs, and opinions. I understood that when I was living only in my thought-based mind, I was limited by these filters and therefore not experiencing the peace of the present moment.

It was a powerful epiphany for me to realize that thinking was at the root of the problem; it caused the clutter. I needed to keep finding ways to quiet my thought-based/intellectual mind and remain in the present moment. This became simple to understand but not easy to practice. I noticed that the less thinking I did, and the more I listened for guidance, the closer I was to my truth. I found this feeling of calm or stillness to be much stronger when I was sitting at my journaling desk, or on one of my many flights, or at the beach watching the waves.

My weekly flights between Florida and New Jersey had become an important alone time that I would always use to journal. I would get so absorbed in my journaling that I would forget all about the activities going on around me on the plane. I felt so engrossed in my spiritual relationship with Chris that I seemed to enter a peaceful and wonderful state of mind that would sometimes last for the entire flight. Many times, I would get startled out of my peaceful place only when the wheels touched down and the plane landed and came to a stop.

In my journaling, I would often ask Chris questions like, *Where did you go? Are you still an individual? Are you still aware? Did your awareness change when you left human form? Where is the mysterious "I" located that seems to be at the core of each of us?*

I felt that if I could get the answers to these questions, I could better understand the peaceful spiritual dimension where both Chris and I reside beyond form. Ever since Chris had died, I'd gone through many periods of uncertainty and would sometimes wonder whether my relationship with him was in my imagination or if I was truly experiencing it. Asking these deeper questions filled my mind with genuine wonder, curiosity, and an openness to know.

Since I always took the first flight out of Palm Beach International at 6:00 a.m., we would arrive at Newark Airport in New Jersey at a very busy time of the morning. We would pull up to the gate, but there was not always a crew ready for us to disembark the plane. I can remember the odd feeling of calm and serenity I would have while standing in the aisle, cramped together with all the other passengers, waiting for the door to open. While many passengers were complaining about the wait, and patience has never been my strong suit either, I still seemed to be in that calm and beautiful place of no thinking mind.

One of the wisest spiritual insights I have ever learned is from the profound adage "to be in the world but not of the world." This short but very deep truism reminds me that while I am in my humanness and can get caught up in the illusions of human thought and ego, my reality is that I am a spiritual being. I have my physical being in this human experience, but my reality is the awareness of my higher spiritual self, which always comes from peace, compassion, and ultimately love. Whenever I walked off the plane after journaling with Chris, I felt that I had been given a glimpse of what it felt like to be "in the world but not of it."

As my day went on, this feeling would fade into the background. Still, I knew that this place of peace was closer to my reality than the illusionary life of reacting to everything going on around me. I understood that there was a definite space of clarity above the clutter of thoughts.

Learning from the Sea

Whether I was in New Jersey or Florida, I loved to take long walking meditations along the beach. I would stare out at the waves and watch how they formed, how they would move almost like they were independent of the great ocean, and then crash on the shore, becoming fully absorbed by the ocean, never to be seen in that exact form again. Philosophers have likened ocean waves to the seeming beginning, middle, and ending of a human life. We all have the experience of being born, living our lives, which can sometimes feel like we are separate from our source, and then reuniting with that source when we die, just as each wave seems to do.

Sometimes, I would pick a wave forming way out in the ocean and think of it as Chris's birth. Chris's "wave" started on December 18, 1981. I would watch that wave "live its life" and then seem to end when it crashed on the shore. For the Chris wave, that would have been December 19, 2004. I would reflect on the fact that for the duration of this wave's life, it had never separated from its source, the vast ocean, even though it looked separate. Separation is impossible for the wave, since it is an emanation of the boundless ocean, derives all of its power from it, and could not exist otherwise.

During these meditations with Chris, I began to understand this life cycle better. Chris's life and my life are both expressions of this great unknown source. Chris's life was a smaller wave that did not keep its form for as long as my life has as a larger wave. But the size or distance a wave travels is insignificant when you see that they are part of the same mighty ocean and are never separate from their source.

One day, I remember sitting on a bench at the Jersey shore in a very lonely place and really missing Chris. I became totally captivated by the ocean, the waves, the sun, the sky, and all of nature around me to the point of forgetting time and even forgetting where I was. After what seemed like a moment but was a couple of hours, I came back from this journey and was still sitting on the bench. My mind was at peace, I had clarity, the sadness had gone, and I felt full of gratitude.

I know during those hours, I went someplace far beyond thinking and became aware of my connection to nature, and even the universe, while being fully aware of my spiritual connection with Chris. My ability to comprehend the mystery of what occurred was beyond my limited thinking mind. But I realized that this meant nothing because, as an unlimited spiritual being, I am part of that mystery.

Thinking Versus Experience

In my search to understand the mystery of life, I was inspired to read a few books on quantum physics. This branch of science takes a huge leap away from analytical thinking and into direct experience. Quantum physics recognizes the power of the observer in an experiment. The observer of the experiment changes the outcome—and so the question becomes: What is really real? Spiritual teachings tell us that we give life all its meaning. Now, it seemed that quantum physics was beginning to prove this spiritual principle.

As I continued my practice of keeping the observer position in my day-to-day life, I began to see that people, places, things, and events stimulate the thinking process in my mind much like sounds stimulate my sense of hearing and sights stimulate my sense of seeing. Buddhists consider the mind to be a sixth sense, and for very good reason. When I related to my thought-based mind as a sensory tool, it helped me create a space around my thoughts just as there is a space between my other senses and what they are sensing.

My other senses do not make me feel ownership over what I hear or see, and they certainly do not change my identity in any way. In other words, when I see beautiful trees and flowers and cars and houses each day, or when I hear birds chirping or listen to music, I don't interpret those things as "mine." Why, then, do I feel ownership of the thoughts passing through the sensor of my mind and feel that they *are* me? This is a key question upon which I began to reflect. I found that the simple act of asking this question often was enough to shake me out of my thoughts.

As an example, I could find myself going down the slippery slope of feeling sorry for myself by allowing my thinking mind to ruminate on the experience of being a father who had lost his only son or brood over how my daughters had lost their big brother. These thoughts could get stimulated when other people were talking to me about their children, or during family events that Chris would have been a big part of, or even at conferences where the next generation was being brought into the business. I had to learn to honor and respect these thoughts as they passed through, but not engage with them or take ownership of them by allowing them to be an identity. Once again, I was learning to better understand what spiritual teachers meant when they said that all events in life are neutral and only we give them their meaning.

I was grateful that I'd had so much time to work with these ideas and practices, which were guiding me closer and closer to my higher self. Chris's death was teaching me so much about life—and I would soon need this wisdom more than ever as my beloved father approached his own transition from his human form.

Chapter 10

A Spiritual Answer to Human Death

Hey Chris,

I saw Gramps yesterday, and I felt that you and me and him were together. His body is still alive, but barely, and I believe that his reality has gone from his local limited form. It still has life, unlike when I saw your body in the hospital, but life at a basic physical survival level only. Seeing him reminds me of what I learned when you died: the reality of life is beyond the human form and must exist at a formless and spiritual level.

Aunt Patty gave me a note written by Ben Franklin that says "human life is an embryo state, a preparation for living. We are not fully born until we die. Why then should we grieve that a new child is born among the immortals?"

Gramps is going to be born as a new child among the immortals. You will be there for him. You have led the way for all of us. Somehow, I got to be picked to be your human dad and then you left to do your work for all of us among the immortals. Help Gramps with his transition. I expect you already have been.

Let's all stay as close as ever and help Gramps move forward with love, peace, and courage.

Love forever and eternity,
Dad

MY DAD WAS, BY far, the most influential person in my life, and never more so than after Christopher's death. He was a pillar of strength and wisdom to whom I could tell everything and anything. In his declining years, he became frailer. He would forget things or repeat himself, and we even had to take his driver's license and car keys away after he had a car accident in which it seemed he may have blanked out. His wife Elaine, who signed birthday and Christmas cards as "Mom E," was by his side every step of the way. My father and Elaine were together for most of my adult life, as my parents had divorced when I was a teenager. They had a deep and loving relationship. My father adored her, they were inseparable, and Elaine feels that spiritual bond to this day.

My sister Patty and I visited with our father often and treasured the deep conversations and humorous moments that occurred on a regular basis. I would look forward to picking my dad up at his home and taking him to the diner, where I would cut up his pancakes and listen to every story he wanted to tell me, soaking up this precious time.

Eventually, Mom E hired an aide to assist my dad at home. Lindsay was a young and vibrant nurse who immediately felt a connection to my dad, truly loved him, and took great care of him. In an early conversation with her, I was amazed to find out she had gone to the same high school as Chris. While they'd moved in different circles, she told me that she always admired his kindness and good nature and the way he was friends with everyone. After this conversation, I felt that her coming into my dad's life at this time was not an accident.

Chris was my father's first grandchild, and I remember the sparkle that came into his eyes the first time he held Chris after he was born. My father took great pride and delight in watching him grow through the years. Their relationship flourished because of their common interests in philosophy and our profession, and Chris idolized his Gramps, finding as much time as possible to spend together. When my father, Chris, and I were together, there was a bond of love, a resonance and understanding, and a connection like our souls had known each other for eternity.

My dad eventually had to move into a nursing home, where Elaine was always by his side, and Patty and I visited him regularly. He was declining physically, and while he did not necessarily like being there and sometimes did not know where he was, he always projected warmth and love and seemed to be even more in touch with his spiritual reality. All of his human inhibitions seemed to fall away. I remember the first time I walked into his room and he was bald. All his life, ever since he was a young professional musician, he had worn a hairpiece that never came off and without which he would never allow anyone to see him. Now, the hairpiece was sometimes on his head, sometimes on the side of his head, and mostly not on his head at all. I am sure it was liberating for him, and he looked more lovable than ever.

My dad was one of the most aware and wise men I have ever known in my life. In his later years, he'd started referring to himself as a "doorman," because his only remaining desire was to serve others by opening their "doors" to understanding. He reached that beautiful time in life where he could shed all his outside identities, from being an accomplished musician to a successful businessman. When someone asked him what he did, he would simply say he was a doorman! Until well into his eighties, friends and family would come to my dad with questions, issues, and life challenges. In his kind, gentle, and loving manner, he would offer them his wise advice and help them open the door to see another way.

During his final weeks, I would sit by his bedside talking to him about our great times together and how much I loved and appreciated them. I recalled the time when he took me with him door to door in our neighborhood, introducing himself and trying to build his new business when I was just a kid. We lived in a lower middle-class Italian area called Down Neck in Newark, New Jersey, and I remember the little Italian ladies inviting us in and offering me cookies while my dad told them about the insurance business he was starting to help the local families.

Later, when I joined him in business, we would often drive to the office together, discussing how we were going to keep growing our business. I felt such excitement for our mutual vision. We also had countless conversations about philosophy, life, and our shared interest in spiritual books. In the evenings, we'd sometimes watch Carl Sagan's *Cosmos* series together, both of us captivated by the stories of our incredible planet and universe. The last time I saw my dad, I sat next to his bed and hugged and kissed him and whispered that it was okay for him to leave and we would all be okay. I flew home to Florida that evening and received a call from Mom E telling me that he had died that night.

I miss my dad but was relieved that he had been released from his broken body and was moving on with his journey. I learned clearly from the experience that Chris and I had to see my father's death from his side and knew there was a way to continue our relationship and stay close to him. The part of my dad that died was only his physical form. Our spiritual partnership would remain unchanged, and we would always meet on the level of consciousness we shared.

Life Has No Opposite

After my father's death, I felt even more certain in my conviction that life is eternal and has no opposite. Birth and death are opposites, but life is unending. We are born into human form and will die out of human form, but our *life* is eternal. Understanding this helped me shift out of a state of limited self-centered emotions, including self-pity, and into an acceptance of death—and even feel a sense of wonder and gratitude. Sadness could still be present, but gratitude was the great healer.

I find it interesting that an estimated 150,000 people around the world die every day. Day in and day out, 150,000 of us human beings die. That's fifty-five million people per year who make their transition. Death touches everyone more often than we realize, whether we're reading about it in the news or it occurs among our friends and family. And except for being born, death is the *only* experience that is guaranteed to happen to every single human living on earth. We celebrate birth, and yet in most cultures we still have no healthy way of dealing with death.

You would think that by now, we would have developed a better way of dealing with this common occurrence. And yet death is mostly spoken of in fearful terms. We fear being death's victim, and we certainly do not want to contemplate our own death. Meanwhile, death can be a great teacher if we view it from our higher self or from a perspective that is beyond this human experience.

The challenge is that this human existence feels very real and the world of form can be all-consuming. We all have family responsibilities, we have our work, we have our home and all of our possessions, we have bills, and we have all of the things we like to do in this world we live in. Death upsets this world of form because none of these things come with us. This seeming end can be very scary from a human point of view—yet this is exactly the reason death is such a great teacher.

On his death bed, Steve Jobs, the billionaire founder of Apple, is quoted as saying, "In the end, my wealth is only a fact of life that I am accustomed to. At this moment, lying on my bed and recalling my life, I realize that all the recognition and wealth that I took so much pride in have paled and become meaningless in the face of my death."

Chris's death made me aware of the reality of life *beyond* worldly forms—beyond the recognition and wealth that Jobs described. Our loving relationship continues to be a significant part of my life long after he has gone from the world. The relationship is carried within me and has nothing to do with Chris's physical existence; I knew the same would be true with my dad.

Love and life are eternal. Birth and death are a very short time and therefore temporary, like all form. Accepting this more spiritual perspective doesn't take away from missing Chris and my dad and feeling sad that they are not here for me to hug, speak with, or just sit with at a diner. We are all human beings with human emotions that need to be acknowledged and allowed to pass through us—and we are also spiritual beings who need to continue to awaken to our spiritual reality, which never dies.

Living in Two Worlds

When I reflected on my father's astute decision to be a humble "doorman" in his last years, I thought of how wise of him it was to drop all other titles and not be centered on himself.

This humility also seemed to be a trait of all spiritual teachers I knew or read about, and I wanted to practice this much more in my own life. I wanted to move beyond my ego being so centered on my needs, wants, expectations, and all the outside world influences.

I found it entertaining to watch my "little self" from the observer position, and sometimes it could even make me laugh out loud. I would catch myself feeling annoyed with someone or something, or complaining about having to go somewhere I didn't want to go. It was interesting and even humorous when I became aware of how often my first reaction was to resist or complain about something that meant very little in the bigger context of my life.

More and more, I felt like I was living in two worlds: the human world of self-centered ego, which was totally involved with people, places, and things and how they affected me, and the much more calm, peaceful, and compassionate spiritual world in which I could accept and allow life to flow. It was always my choice to let my ego or my higher self lead the way.

As I practiced living more of my life from this higher mindset, I found that it became easier to look at people with compassion instead of judgment or reactivity. When my ego was driving, I was always fast to judge people on their looks, the way they communicated, or some other aspect of their persona. I began to recognize this old, ingrained habit pattern more quickly and was able to choose a more open-minded approach. Although I was far from perfect, it felt good not to be stuck in my head judging people and instead enjoy them for who they were. It was also a very welcome change to not be focused on what they thought of me or feel that I had to prove myself to anyone.

I realized when observing myself from this higher place that every person, place, or thing in my life is a teacher, and every experience I have is an opportunity to grow. At some level, all the people in my life have been *chosen* by me. I've decided to spend time with them and to build a relationship. Therefore, the people closest to me are the ones from whom I can learn the most.

When I would meditate or take a walk, I could also feel that I was in a relationship with all of life. People, animals, plants, places, and things felt friendlier, and this entire world was becoming a kinder, more joyful, and beautiful place. It reminded me of the greeting namaste, from the Hindu religion—a beautiful and profound word that translates to "The Divine in me bows to the Divine in you." What a wonderful reminder of the bond we all share. I was so grateful that Chris had opened that window for me.

My Ongoing Search for Answers

The more I observed nature, the more I recognized I was another extension or expression of it. I realized that spirituality and science have many more areas of agreement than disagreement when you look past the terminology. Science says that everything is made up of energy; spirituality says everything is

One and comes from the same Source. That Source has many names in various religions, including God, Father, Jehovah, Allah, and many more. Both science and spirituality point to the same truth: that this "power" is both the origin of all that exists and is contained within all that exists.

I was intrigued by the characteristics that energy takes on through evolving forms. Reason is the newest characteristic in the evolution of form and is displayed only in human beings, allowing us to make informed decisions, solve problems, engage in rational discourse, and understand the world around us. Reason has also ushered in our ability to choose, also known as free will, which is the area in which I was most interested in gaining a better understanding.

One of my first big answers was that we have the power to choose because it is inherent and fundamental in our ability to be aware of ourselves. In other words, I can look in the mirror and see my body and know that this is me or mine. In addition, I am aware of my thoughts and emotions and can observe them and identify them. This ability to be consciously aware of who we are, what we are, and how we feel was a tremendous leap from the level of instinct of the animal. Additionally, our minds have the ability to become aware of *why we are*. This is the great search that I was on. I wanted to become aware of my connection to the Source from which we all emanate that must be based in love, creativity, and oneness.

Another basic principle of science is that energy can neither be created nor destroyed. Therefore, the energy that animates our bodies must continue to exist even after we die. A basic principle of spirituality is that the Source from which we come and are a part of is eternal and so continues after death. Based on these two authorities, it seems apparent that there is continuation after our temporary forms pass away. Until Chris's passing, much of this information sounded good to me, but I only understood it on an intellectual level. Death was an abstract, separate part of life to which I did not pay a lot of attention. Chris's death made it real and transformed these truths into the most important focus of my life.

By far, the most incredible aha moment for me was when I finally embraced what I heard many times: that *we are it*. As they say in *The Matrix*, "You are the one." I could look everywhere outside myself for answers, but all the answers were within because we are *it*. Each one of us is an *individual without separation from our eternal source*. This revelation took my breath away. To be an extension or emanation of this source, and to have awareness and reason, means we have enormous power and responsibility. I found that studying both science and spirituality was providing me more insights and perspectives on both Christopher's and my dad's deaths. Just as importantly, it was giving me a new understanding of the wonder of life.

The Mysterious "I"

Dr. David Hawkins wrote, "Life is an inner subjective experience that includes, but is independent of the physical." In other words, our current existence is an *individual adventure* of that mysterious entity called "I" that is not dependent on form. This has been corroborated by thousands of people who have had near-death experiences. Their bodies were clinically dead and they were fully aware of moving through a wonderful transition but felt they had to return to their human life.

I have never had an NDE, but Hawkins's words felt so encouraging as they supported how I felt that Chris and I could continue our relationship even without him being in a physical body. I felt I was closest to him when journaling, and that connection was beyond my humanness. I felt more confident that what I was experiencing during these times was real and I wasn't merely telling myself what I wanted to hear about our relationship.

Ever since Christopher had died, I'd been pondering the difference between reality and illusion. In philosophy, the definition of reality is "that which exists, independent of human awareness." The definition of illusion is "a perception that is not true to reality, having been altered subjectively in some way in the mind of the perceiver." Chris's death had taught me that the pure and flowing experience of life is reality, whereas our limited thoughts and reactions are what create our unique illusions or experiences. I could feel myself wanting more and more to experience this mysterious oneness and flow of life, and be less identified with the filtered mental illusions that are so distracting.

This concept was illustrated for me one day in a very simple way when I was flying home to Florida. The plane pulled into the gate area and came to a full stop, and the captain turned the engines off. As I gazed out the window at the jetway, I felt the plane moving again, and I thought that was strange since we were already at the gate. It took a few moments for me to realize that the plane wasn't moving at all. It was the jetway being pulled closer to the plane on an angle that created an optical illusion that felt so real to my senses.

As I became aware of this illusion, it dawned on me that this is so much like my life. My body, mind, and all outside forms are moving, and it feels so real, but my spiritual being is not moving at all. My spiritual reality is always in the position of observing. When I am aware of this, it enables me to watch all the activity and stimuli in my outside life and still stay connected to the stillness and calm of my inside life.

I was also seeing how illusions are manufactured by our thought-based minds and do not exist on their own until we put the light of our consciousness on them. The habit of focusing on this level of our mind is exactly what produces the limited illusions we live in. But the mysterious "I," or my awareness, is unchanging in the background.

I felt I was beginning to more clearly understand the illusion of death. When a person leaves their human form, what dies? The body and the brain with its thoughts and emotions dies. The inner subjective awareness does not change—and that is where we remain eternally connected.

Communicating on Other Levels

Christopher's death had done so much to prepare me for my dad's passing. While our human form provides us with a wonderful tool for communicating with each other, and speaking to someone may feel like the most direct way to connect with them, words are inadequate many times. They are not the most effective way to express true feelings. I knew that journaling, and time spent in silence, would become important communication methods with my dad, just as they were with Chris. I started to address my journaling to both Chris and my dad, and while I would have preferred to have them sitting across from me, I felt their presence in a different way. I chose to acknowledge this communication and feel grateful for it. I knew I would stay connected to them as long as I got my thinking out of the way.

As Eckhart Tolle wrote, every human on earth is in the process of unfolding the newest characteristic of consciousness, which is awareness: the universe is becoming aware of itself through us. When I pondered this incredible gift, I felt emotional. As humans, we have the most evolved brains on the planet. Only we have the potential of awakening from our limited illusions and allowing this unlimited consciousness to flow through us. What could be more important?

Then one day several months after my dad's death, I got an email invitation to an Eckhart Tolle retreat at the Omega Institute in Rhinebeck, New York. When I contemplated the possibility of meeting one of my spiritual teachers after studying his books for so long, I registered without hesitation. I knew this was another step in my search for answers and that it would give me the opportunity to get even more connected to Chris and my dad.

Chapter 11

Listening Provides Answers

Hey Chris,

What would I be if not for the story of Steve? What am I, if not a father, husband, son, brother, friend, boss, business owner, provider, spiritual seeker, and all of my opinions, judgments, likes and dislikes and understandings? What would I be?

Would I be more aware of spiritual life? Would I be where you are? Would I care about this human life? Would I have peace? What do I embrace if not all my relationships and the story of me?

If you have not come back to form-based life, then, is this where you are? No personal identification? Does it matter that you were my son for twenty-three years? Did this human life help you in your journey? Does Christopher from 12/18/81 to 12/19/04 mean anything to you? What is the purpose of any human accomplishment if not for raising our level of conscious awareness? Chris, can you guide me in my search?

Love forever and eternity,
Your Dad and Spiritual Partner

ON A CRISP OCTOBER day, I made the two-and-a-half-hour drive from our condo in New Jersey to Rhinebeck, New York, home of the Omega Institute for Holistic Studies. I called Alie, who was home in Florida, and told her I was on my way. She said, "Steve, this is exactly what you need. I am so happy for you and know you will find so many answers you have been seeking." As always, Alie gave me her unconditional support even as we moved forward in our journeys differently. We said I love you to each other and I was on my way.

I had only been to upstate New York a few times, and I was captivated by its feeling of peace and serenity. I often forgot that this huge part of New York State comprises so much beautiful nature, as I spent more of my time in New York City.

As I drove up the countryside with incredible views of the Hudson River and the Catskill Mountains, I took in the beauty and felt my mind becoming calmer and quieter. In the weeks leading up to the Eckhart Tolle retreat, I'd felt a sense of excitement. This was a big step out of my normal comfort zone of buttoned-up business meetings, and I knew it would give me the opportunity to feel even closer to Chris and my dad. I had brought my journal and intended to share every experience with them. In some ways, it felt like the three of us were attending together.

The bed and breakfast I'd booked was in the attic of a funky old house—another new adventure for me. As I walked up the narrow steps and opened the door to my bedroom with its slanted ceiling, I immediately felt an attraction to its charm and history. There was a little alcove area with a writing desk and a window looking over the lake behind the house. I knew right away that this would become my favorite spot. Over the next several days, I would spend hours in the mornings and late evenings journaling to my dad and Chris about everything I was experiencing.

After getting settled into my cozy new home, I took the short drive to Omega. I was instantly enchanted by the beautiful rustic wooden buildings on the 250-acre campus. The whole place radiated a feeling of serenity like I had never felt before. There were many people walking around the grounds. Most were in silence, just taking in all of the simple beauty of this natural setting. I realized I felt so free and liberated because I knew no one, no one knew me, and all my outside world of suits and ties and boardrooms meant nothing here. No one cared what my story was; instead, they accepted me fully as a fellow spiritual student. I felt a release from the exhaustive persona that I spent so much time in and felt myself melting into a state of peace.

I signed in for the retreat and was struck by the warmth and open arms of all the workers and volunteers as well as the feeling of tranquility that was always present. I then made my way to the simple but inviting room where Tolle would be giving his first teaching. The room was already filling with all the retreat participants. The atmosphere was one of reverence and quietude as all were either meditating or enjoying the beautiful sound of silence. It was easy to get into a deeper meditative state in that environment with fellow seekers. I quickly found a seat and savored this time while waiting for Eckhart to appear.

I found it interesting when Tami Simon, Tolle's publisher, started the evening by announcing that participants had the option of experiencing the entire retreat in silence, even wearing a badge to indicate to other people that you did not wish to speak. I knew I wasn't ready to be in silence for the whole week, but I was intrigued. Next, she reminded us to remain in silence when Eckhart Tolle entered the room. This was another unexpected and interesting shift from the many business conferences I have attended, where there was not only lots of conversation but loud applause when the speaker came onto the stage. Instead, the entire room became totally silent. The stillness was palpable and powerful to experience.

Within moments, a thin and gentle-looking man quietly walked onstage to a simple chair with a side table, on which sat a glass of water, a vase with flowers, and a Tibetan bell. He lovingly bowed to the audience, sat down, then stared into space for the next couple minutes. I will never forget the wave of emotion I felt as I sat there. I knew I was in the right place and that he was the one person who could answer the deep questions I'd been struggling with every day. The sense of relief I felt was mixed with a sudden awareness of just how much I'd been carrying. For the first time since Chris died, I was in the presence of a spiritual master whom I knew was fully capable of helping me heal the wounds I hadn't been able to heal on my own.

When Tolle began to speak, he was effortless, eloquent, and powerful. Listening to him, I felt a deep sense of calm. So many of the lessons that I had learned from his writings since Christopher died seemed to be coming through his words, and it felt reassuring to hear. Tolle said that life's challenges can take us to the depths of despair but can eventually make us more present and are necessary for our growth. He also said that being able to step out of thinking and into aware presence is true liberation. He went on to discuss how every experience we have in our lives is the one we need to continue our journey to awakening. And he reflected on life having a bigger context than just this human experience, and that awakening to this context is the true purpose of life.

Tolle explained that this expanded state of awareness offers clarity because it is based in the power of the Now. He said the best indicator that you are coming from this present moment is that it always feels peaceful, no matter the outside circumstances. Emotions like worry, fear, depression, and anger come from thoughts about the past or future; they may feel like the Now, but they're not. The Now is *always* characterized by a place of calm and peace where compassion and love are waiting gently to be acknowledged. As I sat there listening, I felt like Tolle was speaking those words directly to my heart, and I felt the presence of Chris and my dad.

Listening to Understand

Listening to Tolle talk about the Now made me realize how loud my mind could be with all its constant chatter. I recalled a speech I'd once heard at a conference, where a corporate executive gave the advice to always listen with a mindset of wanting to understand rather than with the purpose of formulating a response. "Too often," he said, "we're so busy thinking about what *we're* going to say that we barely even hear what the other person is saying. But when we truly listen, the right response will always be there."

I was so impressed by the speaker and by this comment in particular that I made my way over to him after his speech to ask him more about these remarks. I had met him before but didn't know him very well; now, I found out that he was also an avid meditator. He told me that meditating had taught him the power of truly listening and hearing what people have to say. This listening practice had made a complete transformation in his business and family life, bringing out the best in himself and others. We also spoke about our mutual interest in Tolle's books and how awareness is necessary to practice this level of listening.

Since then, I often observed how the simple act of putting my full focus on the person or people I was interacting with allowed the chatter of my ego to settle down and opened space for me to become aware of my higher self. Interestingly, it was hardest for me to apply this skill with the closest people in my life, my wife and daughters.

It could sometimes feel like I had to bite my tongue until it bled so that I wouldn't react to my opinions or blurt out my words of "wisdom" to them, thinking I already knew what they were going to say. When I focused my mind on really wanting to hear what they were saying, I found that my responses would come from a place of much more understanding and compassion, and that brought with it a sense of happiness and ease within myself.

Thanks to this practice, I realized that in many conversations, I felt like I had to have solutions or answers for the family members or colleagues I was speaking with. Feeling like I had answers made me feel secure, when really I was putting unnecessary pressure on myself and closing my mind to other possibilities beyond my incessant thinking. But now, thanks to years of journaling with Chris and learning to quiet my mind, I was learning to be more comfortable in the uncertain world of "I don't know," which is so much more powerful than the thought-based or intellectual mindset of "I know." When I journaled, I never felt like I needed to have the answers—instead, I asked questions, remained open, and allowed myself to be guided by the flow of consciousness.

All of Life Is a Mystery

At the retreat, it was becoming even clearer to me how entangled I could be with my ego, always wanting to feel the safety of "I know." I felt a sense of control when I could put everything into a neat little package with a bow on it and say, *This is what it is!* or *This is what it means!* or even *This is why it happened!* Yet the only truth about *anything* is that I do not know, unless I have actually experienced it. I may *think* I know something when I reduce it down to its label in language, but language and truth are different things.

Take a tree as an example. We can look at an oak tree and say, *Wow, that is a beautiful oak*. We can analyze how old it might be or how much longer it may live by the size of its trunk or the health of its branches. We can analyze its amazing root system and see how far it expands and supports this majestic tree. We can apply our mental filters, looking through the lens of a conservationist or a logger.

We can also look at an oak tree in the bigger context by resisting giving it labels or explanation, and just feel the joy of the wonder of nature and keep the attitude of a curious child. I have found that when I can look at a tree with this curious attitude, it leads to a feeling of awe as I realize that this enormous expression of life is growing out of the face of the earth. This complex manifestation knows perfectly how to access all the water and nutrients that were necessary to grow from the tiny acorn! Somehow, within that tiny acorn was all of the potential needed to develop into the mighty oak tree.

We have no real understanding of how this mysterious and almost incomprehensible process occurs, yet we still say, "I know," just because we have been taught that an acorn grows into an oak tree. The amazing combination of our Mother

Earth as a birthing organism and the mighty oak form a relationship to create a magnificent form. We have no understanding of how this marvel of nature occurs. Yet, like so much that we think we know, it is based on extremely limited knowledge that our ego-based mind likes to arrogantly speak of as truth—yet by sincerely contemplating the mysteries of nature, or any aspect of life including human behavior, we can discover profound humility.

A Curious Mindset

On breaks between lectures at the retreat, I would walk to the beautiful wooden sundeck outside the quaint little café. Invariably, I'd wind up sitting next to a total stranger and having a wonderful and meaningful conversation. The depth and richness of these discussions, which could sometimes go on for hours, never ceased to amaze me. We would talk about our spiritual interests and experiences with never a word said about what we "do" in the outside world.

Other times, I would take walks around the Omega Institute campus, and I would practice keeping my mind open, quiet, and curious as I took in all of this natural beauty. I could feel the aliveness of the land. It even felt like these grounds were sacred as I kept my mind clear. I avoided naming any of the beautiful vegetation and dropped anything I might know about the amazing and majestic trees I was passing under. Instead, I just appreciated the beautiful and infinitely complex expressions of life and felt immersed in awe.

At night, this would continue as I walked into the yard of my bed and breakfast and gazed at the stars, letting myself feel just how vast the universe really is. I was so fascinated by the fact that our Milky Way Galaxy has over two billion suns like ours and that there are over two trillion galaxies in our observable universe. Just the attempt to wrap my head around this fact while taking in the dark country sky would open me up to further awe and wonder. I couldn't help but feel gratitude for being a part of this wonder, and I also felt so grateful to Christopher and my dad for leading me here.

I was beginning to grasp that everything has a purpose, and that life emanates and unfolds in a state of perfection—including my own life. The question then occurred to me: *Does that make me a victim of this unfolding universe, as all is fate or destiny?* And the answer came almost as quickly: *No, I am a victor, because I am consciously aware and therefore have choice as to how I will respond to its unfolding.*

Beyond Choice

As I continued practicing having an open and curious mind in my day-to-day life, I felt that I was beginning to experience something beyond choice. It seemed that when I was able to get totally "out of the way," I didn't even have to choose. Instead, I could be guided to the right place at the right time, or to say the right thing. My experiences at the retreat had shown me that I would always sit next to exactly the person I needed to meet and have exactly the conversation I needed to have.

Some days, I had also felt guided to sit at one of the silent tables. Although my choice would have been to socialize at one of the other tables, my experience of eating with a group of people in total silence was powerful. With no need to speak or even introduce myself, my mind was clear to be more present. I remember how the taste of the food was so much more delicious. I ate more slowly and more purposefully, and the unspoken feeling between all of us at the table was one of joy and peace.

I realized that when Christopher died, the deep love that I have for him is what guided me to see his death another way. My need to feel him, communicate with him, and continue a relationship with him was the power that opened me to the guidance beyond choice. Guidance was always available from a higher level, or my higher self, when I allowed space for it and trusted it. This guidance came more from my heart than my head and seemed closer to truth than mere choice.

I found myself doing things that might not be what I would have chosen, but they seemed to lead to something I needed to experience. This had the effect of making every situation an opportunity for my maximal learning. The deaths of my son and my father taught me that there is a learning opportunity and even a blessing in every life experience and that all of life is a gift on my journey to awakening.

I found myself continually pondering the profound statement of the masters, that "I, of myself, do nothing, but the power within does all the work." When I surrendered to the flow of life, I felt liberated from my fear-based, mind-manufactured concepts, beliefs, opinions, and judgments. I was finding that true freedom means living in the reality of uncertainty. This is my natural state.

My relationship with Chris had forced me to look deeply into the truth of this reality. I began to look for the meaning in everything—all of my relationships with people, places, and things. A whole new dimension of beauty had entered my life because I was allowing myself to see beyond the surface to the mystery beyond. I began to accept people and things for who and what they were and let them out of the boxes I had put them in. This led me to feeling more compassion for all and living more in the Now—everything that Tolle was teaching.

Integrating the Life Lessons

On the final morning of the retreat, Eckhart closed his remarks by telling us that all our experiences and all that we had learned at this retreat were within us now, part of our essence. As we headed home, he urged us to remember that this was the beginning of bringing more conscious presence into our lives. When he and his wife Kim ended the conference and stood together saying goodbye, I felt so much peace and love within me and for everyone that I could not stop tears from running down my face.

I eventually left the room and sat on a grassy hill with many other students outside of the building where Eckhart and Kim were staying, knowing that they were leaving the campus and wanting to give a final wave goodbye. They came out and got into a waiting golf cart. There was absolute silence and a feeling of serenity as they bid farewell. I walked around the campus for hours before leaving and just bathed in this sense of peace.

When I got home from the retreat, I felt so inspired about life and was even more committed to my spiritual practices of meditating, journaling, and treating all with love and compassion. Coming back into the real world of day-to-day life was a bit jolting, as the demands of business and family life were waiting for me. In addition, all the influences of people, social media, and the news were back in my life. I could have easily allowed myself to be pulled back into old habits and reactions and get caught up in too much thinking and opinions. But I was determined, and that meant taking a few simple steps to guard my newfound peace from these distractions.

I decided to completely stop watching TV news and to only use the internet for information I needed and for electronic communication. I would not use social media. I would not read or listen to negative ads or articles, and I would not engage in divisive or disheartening discussions. I would purposely seek out and spend time with people and activities that were uplifting. I continued to read books by spiritual authors and generally operated from a context of making choices that enhanced my spiritual journey and desire for peace in my life.

Thanks to these practices, I felt that I was turning another corner. I was still asking many questions about Christopher's death, but these questions were no longer about the "why" of the experience. Instead, they were all about how I could continue to grow. It seemed to me I had reached a commitment level and mindset where life was pulling me toward this higher path—although life would soon surprise me yet again.

Chapter 12

Humility, Gratitude, and Willingness

Hey Chris,

I love you so very much. There is very little in my life that has not been affected by you and our experience, and I'm proud of that. You help me focus on my spiritual awareness so I can experience spiritual growth while in this human form. It seems that so much of humanness is based in the ego and in fear-based survival habits which are no longer necessary. I am finding much more strength in humility, which is a trait you exemplified in your human life. Thanks to our ongoing relationship, I am also finding gratitude for all that life has to offer, and a willingness to surrender to the flow of life. These seem to be the keys to growth and enjoyment during my human experience.

Love forever and eternity,
Dad

LIFE CHANGED NOW THAT both of my parents had passed away. My mom had died many years ago, when Chris and Dani were young and Alex was less than one year old. She used to visit us every Saturday morning and bring over hot bagels. She always had some little gift of candy or a tiny toy for the grandchildren she adored. She was our biggest fan, we could do no wrong, and her dying at a relatively young age left a hole in our lives. Now that my father had also died, the importance of continued spiritual growth became even more apparent to me, as I was now one of the elders in my family.

Chris's death was now several years in the past, and it seemed that time was beginning to move more quickly. Alex was growing up fast; before Alie and I knew it, she had graduated from high school and enrolled at the University of Tampa in Florida, majoring in communications. Alex was ready to spread her wings, and she enjoyed the move from her small private school and the small-town feel of Delray Beach. She soon blossomed and began to thrive in the hustle and bustle of city life in Tampa and at her excellent university. She joined a sorority and became an officer, made many new friends, and integrated herself fully into her new life. Alie and I, on the other hand, had to deal with our empty nest, no longer having our lives revolve around Alex and her swim meets and social life.

Dani was well into being a grown-up, staying in Philadelphia after graduating from an excellent culinary college. She was managing a bakery and dessert shop in the middle of the city and had always dreamed of having her own business. Chris, in his wisdom, had made Dani and Alex the beneficiaries of the life insurance he had bought and was given in his benefits package from work, and Dani used part of that money to buy a house. She lived in one room and rented the others to a few of her friends.

When Dani was approaching age twenty-four, which was the age at which Chris had died, Alie and I experienced a subtle but persistent sense of worry. As this important birthday got closer, we felt a sense of apprehension and even fear, and looked forward to when our daughter would be our first child to surpass that age.

The day that Dani officially became older than her big brother was emotional for all of us. She would now be having all the experiences that he never had. When he was alive, she had always been able to rely on him to be there for her as a devoted older brother. Getting married, having children, and moving fully into adult life without her brother's guidance was not going to be easy. To add some lightness to this serious milestone, she would sometimes joke that she was one of very few people who could say they were the youngest child, the middle child, and now the oldest child in a family. However, the truth is that we all still look at Chris, in our ongoing relationship with him, as the oldest child, and as much a part of our family as he ever was.

One day when Dani and I were having one of our lunches in Philadelphia, we began to discuss her dream of owning her own bakery and coffee shop. She still had money left from her inheritance from Chris, and she had also built equity in the house she owned.

"You know, Dani," I said, "your mom and I would love it if you moved to Florida. If you come down to Delray, we could be a big help to you opening your own coffee shop."

It took a bit of convincing, but she agreed that this could be a perfect new start. A few months later, the Daisy Coffee Shop and Bakery was born in Lauderdale by the Sea.

Running a food service business proved to be exhilarating, exciting, hectic, and stressful in equal measures. We all learned how tough the food business can be. Dani was working sometimes more than fifteen hours per day. This lasted for almost three years until we finally decided to sell the business. It was an accelerated education in the world of small restaurant ownership. We have newfound respect for anyone who succeeds in that business, and we were happy to put that dream behind us.

Moving Forward

Our two beautiful daughters, who seemed to be little girls only yesterday, were grown up and living their adult lives. Alex was in Tampa working in marketing for the Tampa Sports Authority and Dani was now managing a Nordstrom restaurant. They knew that the heartbreak and sadness of losing their beloved big brother could always surface, but they now had experience and tools to work with. They knew that these feelings would come, and they would go, and that focusing on their ongoing relationship with Chris and his continued journey would keep them moving forward.

Alie and I also moved forward on our paths and realized more than ever how much we cherished our time together and the support we provided each other. Alie never looked her age and had built a busy life around playing competitive tennis in southern Florida. I, on the other hand, was quickly going gray and feeling a bit older, but I tried to keep it together with running and some gym work. We would take long walks together, enjoyed our discussions about life, and regularly went to our favorite Delray Beach restaurants.

I felt so grateful that my life had been blessed with a loving marriage that was able to endure the tragedy of a child's death, when so many marriages fail after this type of crisis. Alie and I both knew how much energy we put into handling this unimaginable experience. We knew the toll it took on all of us as well as the strength we gained. Living through this experience together had created a bond of understanding between us. It also made us think about our own mortality, knowing that we would not be here forever. While we viewed death very differently now, we did not want any other loved ones to die, including ourselves.

Reflecting on my life to this point, and especially on the ways that Christopher's death had changed my life, I realized there were three virtues I continually had to acknowledge and apply. They are humility, gratitude, and willingness. I found these to be the healing levels of consciousness that led me to new dimensions of understanding in every aspect of life. They open the door and allow the essence of truth and love to shine through, and I work on practicing them every day.

Humility

I have found that deep and genuine humility is a quality that requires steely discipline and vigilance. The ego has such a strong hold on us, with its origins dating back to the early days of humanity, when its survival skills enabled us to exist day to day. The ego helped us with its self-preservation and self-centered focus, but since it is fear based, it cannot take us any further. The need to develop the higher love-based energy in the attribute of humility is critical to moving forward in our individual lives and in our society.

Interestingly, I have noticed that it is easy to act humble, and even self-deprecating, but this is not real humility. I found that true humility requires being fully present within myself and with others. When I was not fully in the moment, I could feel an unbalance that came from overthinking, looking for approval, or trying to impress, which is all ego based. When I am aware and engaged in the moment, I find that words flow effortlessly, there are no scattered thoughts, and I provide value selflessly. None of my needs get attached, including looking for a thank-you, and I am much more at peace. Not only that, but when I came from humility, I would find myself saying what someone needed to hear or doing the right thing at the right time. True humility comes from deep inner strength and never needs to promote or defend itself.

I experienced this very clearly when I gave the eulogy at the services for my father. There was a large group of family and friends, and I remember feeling totally at peace that morning and the entire day. My remarks had the sole purpose of honoring my father and his life and acknowledging what he meant to me and so many others. I had an outline of what I wanted to say and even played a recording of one of his records from when he was a musician. But when I began to speak, it felt that it was just my dad and me in that room. I saw everyone very clearly, and the feeling was warmth, calm, and peace. It felt like my dad and I were side by side, having one of our conversations. Afterward, so many people thanked me and said that they also felt a sense of calm and peacefulness. I had a deep sense of humility for the words and feelings that came through me and felt glad that they may have been able to help others.

I was starting to find that real clarity and courage come from the enormous strength of conviction that only humility can provide. I remember watching the movie about Ghandi and being so moved by his calm devotion to peace that gave him such great power. Humility is a quiet and yet tremendously strong, purpose-driven energy that allows our higher self to do the work.

Humility is not necessarily taught to us in school or in business, but I have found it to be a vital attribute for success in life. When I focused on providing genuine value and being humble, there could always be a win-win for all. In my various roles of father, husband, brother, friend, and businessman, I found that leading with real humility and looking for nothing in return allowed others to respond with more compassion as well. Humility opens the way to healing relationships, as well as healing our hurts and suffering, and carries with it tremendous strength.

Gratitude

As the years went by, I found that time lessened the strength of the feelings of sadness and missing Chris, although they never went away. Surprisingly, I was slowly realizing how grateful I felt for all that this experience had taught me. I felt I was becoming a better, possibly wiser person, with a richer understanding of life. I remember hearing Stephen Colbert, whose father and brother died in a plane accident when he was ten, say in an interview, "If you are grateful for your life, then you must be grateful for all of it; you can't pick and choose." I realized that while I never would have chosen the biggest tragedy and challenge in my life, it had become my greatest opportunity for learning and transformation.

My relationship with Chris has given me eyes to see more clearly on this human journey. By necessity, it makes me much more aware and focused on the spiritual dimension of my life, as this is where our relationship exists. This is a gift and a blessing, and it makes all the difference in the joy and happiness I experience every day. And, for that, I could not be more grateful.

I find that it is relatively easy to remind myself to count my blessings and be grateful for things like my family that I love, the country I live in, my friends who enrich my life, and even for the food I have to eat and the air I breathe. But extending gratitude for the challenges of life goes far deeper. It is the difference between appreciation for the good of life and the potential for transformation when we find gratitude in the most difficult times.

I remember reading a book by Harvard Professor Steven Pinker titled *The Better Angels of Our Nature*, which gave so many reasons to live our lives with gratitude. Dr. Pinker made the point, supported by enormous amounts of empirical data, facts, and evidence, that we live in the greatest time in the history of humanity. It may sometimes be hard to believe, based on the nightly news, that we are living in the very best of times. Dr. Pinker demonstrated that when it comes to war, crime, drugs, the murder rate, and many other conditions in society, we are doing exceptionally well compared to all previous generations. Just looking at the wars of the twentieth century and the tens of millions of people who were killed during that hundred-year period is staggering. Even though we live in the best of times, the influence of news and social media can make us feel otherwise. However, data proves that our society is learning and moving forward, and that gives us all so much to be grateful for.

I often think about how fortunate I am for all the resources provided by our modern times, including access to so much spiritual information via books, YouTube, and the internet that we did not have only a short time ago. Technology allows for instant answers and research on any topic I may have interest in, from music to history and all of science and the arts. The inventions of the last one hundred years have given us an exponential increase in the quality of our lives. And yet the deepest gratitude that I feel is for all of my life experiences, including the challenges and difficulties, and especially for the awareness to see the lessons in all of them each and every day. This level of gratitude helps me enjoy my life through the good times and the tough times and feel the joy of being.

Willingness

My experience with Christopher taught me the importance of willingness, or what could be called surrender or letting go. I'm not sure I can say I learned it voluntarily, because it seemed I was pushed into it by the need to get out of misery. Chris's death was such an unthinkable and catastrophic event that my mind had no answers to give. I was in a place of pain and suffering of a kind I had never experienced before. Somehow, by the grace of God, I realized that with no place to go, there had to be another way. In hindsight, I see that when I let go, it immediately opened some lightness and space where I felt hope. I knew that I of myself did not have tools to handle this situation, but that those tools existed in this life, and maybe all I had to do was stay out of the way. I wasn't sure of much, but I knew there was another way, and that way could lead me out of misery and maybe even bring me peace.

Genuine willingness lifted me out of the pain of resistance. When Christopher died, I was in the deep suffering of resistance, denial, and blame of all outside events. But when I realized there was another way, that gave me the inspiration to pursue it. For me, that meant reading spiritual books voraciously, journaling, meditating, and looking within. I began to have the courage and willingness to quiet my mind and ask for guidance. This was a direct confrontation to my ego-based mind, and it was a daily commitment to be open and let go. Slowly, my willingness began to weaken the energy of resisting the flow of life.

The Mechanism of Letting Go

In those years, I always seemed to be reading a David Hawkins book. One day, I landed on a page that gave me great guidance in understanding willingness, surrender, and what I was going through. He wrote, "Letting go involves being aware of a feeling, letting it come up, staying with it, and letting it run its course without wanting to make it different or do anything about it." He went on to say, "The technique is to be with the feeling and surrender all efforts to modify it in any way. Let go of wanting to resist the feeling. It is resistance that keeps the feeling going."

As I read this short explanation of surrender, it occurred to me that being open to my feelings with willingness and intention to let go would create the space for the process of healing to take place. I did not have to do anything else. Indeed, the truth is I have no idea how to heal my own suffering. But if I use the "master levers" of willingness and intention, the process of healing will occur by way of surrendering to a power greater than myself.

In this process, I also found it helpful to remember that no matter what I may be going through, *life is not here to torture me but to teach me*. I know this is the truth, and with this mindset, I always felt encouraged that I could reframe every single experience in my life as a learning opportunity. When I feel sad, angry, or guilty, or whether the reaction is creating an experience of feeling insecure or unworthy, I can make another choice when I am observing. By surrendering to whatever I am experiencing, life itself heals me, and the temporary emotions of sadness and fear move away.

By this time in my journey, I was consciously using the process of surrender when I felt sad about Chris. I had so much experience with sadness, from the early days when it was so gripping and it overpowered my mind, to eventually recognizing that sadness was not going to kill me and there is another way. Now when I feel sadness, I just stay with the feeling. I do not fear it in any way, nor do I add to it with thoughts or discuss it with anyone. If anything, I will write about the feeling in my journal, or simply allow it to pass through. With the tools of intention, willingness, and surrender, the sadness will evaporate within a relatively short amount of time.

As I practice using the technique of letting go with other feelings, I have noticed that my ego-based mind seems to crave complication and complexity. It wants to admire the problem and get more "juice" out of discussing it and dwelling on it and building stories about it, even if it hurts. I have learned that the real "work" consists of staying vigilant every day to allow life to flow, let go of judgments and opinions, and generally make choices toward compassion and understanding.

I fell short often, but I would catch myself more quickly than in the past. I was getting better at observing how the distress, whatever it may be, has no power itself. It did not exist except in my mind, when I chose to focus on it or even manufacture it. I had complete power to pull the plug on it by simply making another choice. However, the attraction of the ego and the strange satisfaction I could get from the drama it could spin meant that this simple process was anything but easy.

This drama was even stronger when I felt a sense of righteousness about my opinion or judgment. The temptation to react was strong, but I would remember to ask myself, *Would I rather be right or happy?* I noticed how often I wanted to be right. Sometimes, I would let go a thousand times if necessary, repeating the letting-go process every time my mind came up with another rationalization, excuse, or justification. I would just observe my ego's desire to be right until I reconnected with my desire for peace.

The peaceful feeling I would get after successfully letting go seemed to come from the release of the pressure of holding on to my wanting to be right. Letting go allows the energy of that emotion to transform into the energy of freedom, like a weight has been lifted. By not suppressing, denying, or fearing my own feelings, I could observe them and then embrace them as blessings that have given me awareness of a part of me that needs to be gently released. The best barometer for me is the feeling of lightness.

Love Is the Only Reality

As Alie and I settled into our lives as empty nesters, I would often have quiet time in Delray when she was playing tennis. I would sit in my backyard staring at palm trees in contemplation. As I drifted into this beautiful stillness, it would occur to me that love is what we must be if we are all an emanation from a Source that is all giving and everywhere present. And if that is the case, then my true essence must be love, and I could share my love by giving back to life by accepting its flow and having compassion for all. The reality of love lives within everyone—it always has and always will.

I remember a profound statement I heard that has been quoted by many spiritual masters; that *we move from living life to life living us.* This statement tells me to accept myself fully for who I am. I am a creation of the one and only Source of all life. When I would remind myself of this, I would begin to feel tremendous gratitude that I have been given the enormous gift of being aware. I am part of this amazing universe, and all its power is here for me to live a life of peace and joy.

My "job" is to stay out of the way and simply enjoy my continued awakening to the mysterious power that lives within all—while savoring the everyday life I share with my family. This is also when I feel closest to Christopher.

It seemed to me that Alie and I had a lot to look forward to as we approached retirement age. We had a beautiful home and two beautiful daughters who would someday have families of their own; after several decades of marriage, our bond was stronger than ever. Yet the work of surrender was never done, and I would soon be faced with one more heartbreaking and life-changing event where I needed every tool that Chris's death had taught me.

Chapter 13

A Willingness to Be Guided

Hey Chris,

After all these years, there are times when I still feel a strange sense of fear or surprise when I think about having a son who died. I wonder if this is because I have such a strong sense of our ongoing love and relationship? It would be nice to have it all—a physical, mental, and spiritual relationship—but if I can only have one, I am so grateful to have clarity about the eternal spiritual bond we share. I am open to seeing even more and deepening my understanding of the spiritual dimension that is our true reality and only existence. Let's learn and understand together.

Love forever and eternity,
Dad

EVER SINCE WE BOUGHT our home in Delray Beach, Alie had enjoyed playing tennis almost every day. She was in great shape and was close friends with the other women at her racquet club. But in the winter of 2017, she noticed a strange pain on the right side of her upper body. She assumed she had pulled a muscle and continued to play through the pain. When it remained persistent, she decided to go to a doctor. Due to her good health and no family history of any diseases, they diagnosed her with an intercostal muscle strain with no further testing. The treatment was to rest it, ice it, and stretch those muscles regularly. Alie was anxious to get back to playing. Yet she found that no matter what she did, the pain kept getting worse, and she would find herself getting short of breath when she never used to be.

Late that spring, around Mother's Day, we headed up to New Jersey, where we would stay for the summer. Alie continued to feel pain and it wasn't getting better, so I said, "Let's just go to a doctor up here and see what they say."

Both Alie and I had been healthy our whole lives and didn't even have a regular physician. We were referred to someone not far from us, and he gave Alie a complete physical and felt she was okay. But because she had had a small melanoma removed from her arm a few years before, he recommended a CAT scan to be safe.

Alie went in for the CAT scan. The next day, the doctor called me. "Mr. Ferrara, the results don't look good. I want to get Alie into Sloane Kettering Cancer Center as soon as possible for further analysis." Within a couple days, we had an appointment to see one of their top oncologists.

On the morning of the appointment, we got there early and waited for the oncologist in his examination room. He came in, sat down, introduced himself, and said, "Mrs. Ferrara, I'm sorry to say that you have Stage IV lung cancer."

Alie and I were shocked and didn't even know which questions to ask. He told us that he and his team would discuss options for treatment and get back to us within a day or so. In hindsight, I realize how little I understood about this diagnosis. I thought that Alie would go in for some treatments and be back to her healthy self and playing tennis very soon. Alie, on the other hand, understood the severity of the diagnosis. As we walked to the car, she turned to me in tears and said, "I feel so bad for Dani and Alex." At that point, I assumed that this was an understandably emotional response and maybe even an overreaction, but I soon learned I was wrong.

The oncologist called me the next morning to say that the CAT scan showed that Alie's cancer was very advanced. While they stopped short of saying that her prognosis was terminal, they told us that, due to her otherwise healthy body, they felt that an aggressive plan of chemotherapy, radiation, and immunotherapy might have an effect. However, this treatment needed to start immediately.

I had a colleague who had many doctors as clients across the country. I contacted him, and on that same day, he had the two top oncologists at large hospitals in Cleveland and Houston contact me. I sent them Alie's CAT scan. They both agreed that her situation was dire and that this aggressive plan might be the only course of action.

I told Alie that the Sloane Kettering doctors had developed a treatment plan, and it would start the next day. We had the very tough conversation with our daughters, and they immediately acted. Dani's workplace had a twelve-week leave of absence program available for a family emergency, of which she took advantage. Alex came to New Jersey from Tampa, and we were all together during this very difficult time for Alie. Overnight, we were thrust into the world of aggressive cancer treatment, and it quickly depleted Alie's body. In just a few weeks, she had become a shadow of herself. She lost weight, her muscle wasted away, and she went from a thriving, independent life to being almost totally debilitated.

Although Dani, Alex, and I were not cut out to be nurses or caregivers, as that had always been Mom's role, we nevertheless found ourselves giving Alie needles, making sure she had the many medications she needed, and keeping her on an oxygen machine even while taking her back and forth to Sloan Kettering Hospital in New York, a harrowing three-hour drive. One early morning, while I was giving her one of her needles, Alie looked at me with soft and loving eyes and said, "Steve, you have always been my husband I love dearly. Your caring for me makes me appreciate even more what we have, and you should always be happy." After spending so many years being the rock of our family, Alie was now in the position of letting Dani, Alex, and me play that role for her.

Despite our best efforts, Alie's condition worsened, and she was in and out of the hospital multiple times. Her doctor mercifully put her in a local hospital for what would be the last time, where we did not have to drive into New York City every day. Dani, Alex, and I stayed with her around the clock. Alie used every last bit of her strength to try to get up and walk the hospital hallways to show that she might qualify for physical therapy and ultimately be released back home. But she weakened further and even began to fall into unconsciousness due to the drugs she needed to stay out of pain.

It was clear to the doctors and hospital staff that Alie's time was coming, and yet I told myself there was still a chance that she would recover. I even demanded a meeting with her lead doctor to express my concerns for this plan of treatment. The doctor told me they had decided to go with this aggressive plan due to Alie's young age and health, but that normally, for someone with such advanced disease, the only option would have been hospice. My mind didn't want to accept the unimaginable fact that Alie would soon be gone, and so I clung to hope, even though for the first time, I was beginning to acknowledge the inevitable.

The following morning, Dani, Alex, and I were in our now-familiar positions around Alie's bed. She had been unconscious for several hours when she suddenly opened her eyes, sat up a little, and started singing quietly to us. "I love you more than you'll ever know; I love you more than the trees that grow." We all started crying, and we all hugged while listening to these beautiful words and the deep love in her voice. Then just as soon as she had woken up, she lay back down and fell unconscious again.

That day, I had a meeting with the hospice staff, who told me how that service worked. I was still in denial but agreed that this seemed to be the right plan of action. It had only been seven weeks since Alie's original diagnosis. There had not been a moment when we were not in crisis mode. It all felt surreal.

It was only later that evening, after Dani, Alex, and I had been at the hospital day and night for several days straight, that the young nurse who had been by our side the whole time pulled me aside and said, "Why don't you guys take a break and go out to dinner?"

She was so much wiser than her twenty-three years and knew it was Alie's time. She whispered, "Sometimes a person won't let go unless they're alone." Dani, Alex, my niece Caity, and I reluctantly walked to a restaurant near the hospital. We didn't want to leave Alie, but we were all exhausted and it seemed like the right thing to do.

With heavy hearts, we quietly sat down for dinner. We decided to make a toast to our beautiful Alie, and we all ordered her favorite drink, a lemon vodka and tonic. Minutes after our toast, the nurse called to tell us that Alie had passed. We left some money on the table for the drinks and immediately ran back to the hospital, where we all cried with Alie's lifeless body for a very long time.

Alex, Dani, and I stayed close together in our home in New Jersey for the rest of the summer, with many of our friends and relatives visiting us every day and night. Dani resumed her work schedule and went back to her own home. I asked Alex if she wanted to take the next semester off from university and stay in New Jersey with us. "Dad," she said, "I've thought about it, but I think it will be better for me to get back to my routines at school." I started going back to my office, building new domestic habits to run my life, and getting used to the new normal of not being part of a couple.

Honoring Each Other's Journey

Alie had been the most loving wife and mother and the cornerstone of our family. We'd grown up together since we met at age twenty-one, and our lives were completely intertwined. I loved being at each other's side for almost forty years. We had three wonderful children and built a life that we all loved. I can also say, without a doubt, that if not for Alie, I could not have moved forward in my life in a healthy way after Chris's death. She was so strong, so clear on what we had to do, and so loving to our daughters and myself in every way, putting her own feelings aside.

I felt that Alie had died only after she knew that she had done her very best to put Dani, Alex, and me in a place where we would be okay to move forward without her. She was a mom and wife first and foremost her entire life and always focused on our family as her top priority. Because she always sacrificed her own needs, I sometimes wondered if she had given herself enough time, attention, and space to allow herself to heal after our beautiful son passed away. She seemed to carry that deep pain within her and couldn't let it go enough to accept or find peace with it. We both respected the differences in our ways of handling this unimaginable tragedy, and in fact, this respect had brought us even closer; still, I often wished I could have carried her on my journey and spiritual quest.

My hope and prayer every night was that Alie and Chris might be once again traveling together, and that Alie had found the joy and peace she so deserved. Dani once told me that her mom and I had very different ways of dealing with grief and even with life. She appreciated those distinct differences that we offered her and Alex, and they knew exactly which one of us to come to depending on the issue. Our different qualities and approaches complemented each other and made us stronger together. Now, on my own, I would do my best. While the sadness and loneliness I felt with Alie being gone could be agonizing at times, I also found comfort in supporting her in her ongoing journey, no matter what form it took.

Miracles Are a Normal Part of Life

After Alie died, I continued to attend my *A Course in Miracles* study group, where I found encouragement and inspiration from a committed group of fellow spiritual seekers. According to *ACIM*, a miracle is "a change in perception"—or what could be considered a new paradigm. In any moment, I can choose to change my perception or reframe how I view a person or event, and that changes my entire life experience. I can remember so many times sitting down to journal with Alie and feeling so lonesome and sad. I would allow those feelings to stay with me while I observed them, did not engage with them, and just kept journaling.

This simple choice to stay present and keep writing would change my mindset and, like a miracle, I would find myself totally engrossed and enjoying this time with Alie: sharing a dream or experience I had, asking her questions about her new journey, and so many other topics. I remember asking her whether she still had feelings and questions like, *Have you taken on another form? What do you think about? Are you with Chris? What is it like without the senses of a body?* And *Do thoughts and opinions even exist wherever you are?* There were times I felt an answer and times I did not, but choosing to allow a stream of consciousness to flow always had the effect of changing my perception. That change shifted my entire experience from loneliness to thoroughly enjoying my time with Alie.

In line with this, I was also practicing embracing stillness and listening for guidance. Our home was so silent when I woke up in the morning and only had my two shih tzus, Lilly and Oliver, waiting for me. Without Alie there to talk to first thing in the morning, I felt a strange sense of insecurity and even some fear about not having a partner to express myself with. I journaled about this often and decided to start an

ACIM habit of asking each morning, *What should I do? Where should I go? What should I say? And to whom?* These questions helped me clear my mind and approach my day with openness, which then helped me feel more comfortable in the new uncertainty of my life. I found that this approach often had the added benefit of leading me to the right place at the right time and having unexpectedly meaningful conversations with colleagues, employees, and most everyone I met. I could only feel grateful for these small miracles, and they seemed to happen more often as I stayed out of the way.

Settling into my new life, I would remind myself that all of life is a classroom, and I am a student whose responsibility is to keep an open mind and look for the learning opportunity in all experiences. Like Chris's death, Alie's death changed everything, and I needed to stay open to what life was teaching me. In doing so, I found myself becoming more caring and compassionate with everyone I met. I was becoming an even more involved father to my daughters, and I was practicing reframing the challenges in my life as blessings to learn from.

Just like after Christopher's death, I was determined that the purpose of this traumatic experience could not be to feel sorry for myself but to accelerate my spiritual growth. I knew that the world and all its events, including the death of my beloved wife, were happening without error. I also knew, more than ever, that I give life all its meaning by how I choose to view it, and that gives me my life experiences. Taking that total responsibility for my choices is where all of my strength resides. Coming from this higher understanding was making my world a beautiful and loving place again, even after Alie died. This is what I felt was being expressed in *A Course in Miracles* when it said, "Miracles happen every day; change your perception and you'll see them all around you."

We Choose Our Spiritual Partners for Our Growth

Many of the spiritual masters that I have read and studied agree that our souls choose the people with whom we will travel together in this lifetime. That includes our parents, our spouses, and our family and friends. We choose our "soul partners" based on our levels of consciousness. I have always felt this way about Christopher and my dad while they were here in form, and even more now that they are formless. Now that Alie had transitioned, I was beginning to feel the depth of our relationship as soulmates and that our journey together may have begun before this human experience and would continue beyond.

It occurred to me that choosing our "spiritual partners" is the optimal way for us to grow to become aware of our true reality. Looking at all my relationships from this deeper place enables me to embrace the love, as well as the lessons, that I can learn through the experiences we share. As I looked beyond my thoughts, emotions, and senses that limit me to humanness, I could feel a closer bond with everyone in my life. Staying in this state of mind required me to be vigilant about letting go of my fears, worries, opinions, likes, and dislikes. I felt closer to my truth, which can only be love, when I was able to surrender like this.

I noticed that when I observed life in this more spiritual context, I could feel and know that my human life is only a small part of the journey I am on. It was clear to me that life must be more than this short human experience of pleasures and struggles. This higher view also gave me assurance that when Alie left her human journey, there was no question that our relationship could continue as it had with Chris.

I felt closest to this understanding when I gave myself quiet time where thought and mental chatter could slow down. This peaceful and blessed silence was becoming more and more important to me and was when I could deeply feel that all of life is connected at a spiritual level. This new awareness helped me know that we never truly lose anyone to death, and it helped me relate to life in a more complete way.

The Journey with No Distance

The spiritual teacher Anthony de Mello once wrote, "The spiritual quest is a journey without distance. You travel from where you are right now to where you have always been." I felt that this profound statement acknowledged what I had been learning at Tolle retreats about the power of Now. If there is no past or future except for what our minds manufacture, then living in the Now is living in eternity, or what has been called *allness*. Therefore, whether we are in our bodies or beyond, we are all still connected. I certainly longed to hold Alie's hand again or have a conversation, but this understanding gave me the comfort of knowing we were still together.

Now that Chris, my mom and dad, and Alie had all moved on in their journeys, I was more determined than ever to understand life. I started with the recognition that I am a spiritual being having a human experience. This truth opened the door to realize that I have never been separated from the source of love that created me. This then led me to ask why it is so hard at times to live my life from this place.

The answer seemed to be that my ego, with its judgments, beliefs, and opinions, made me feel separated, and this took away my innate sense of peace. I decided to make choices within the context of what gives me joy, fulfillment, and peace, to the best of my ability.

I used this context in my relationship with Alie. While I missed her warmth and touch, I knew that we had something special that was real and forever. I could allow myself to feel joy because I let go of any regrets and guilt I carried in our relationship and allowed myself to feel the love within me that I had always shared with her. This new context began to change my life in every way as I either made choices that would give me peace or adapted to the people or situations when I could not choose differently. I often repeated to myself the wise proverb, *Let there be peace, and let it begin with me.*

I felt that this journey with no distance was a journey to remember "home." Home is our spiritual reality, a place we have never left, where there truly is no birth or death—only life. I could be a conscious participant in this journey, or I could be lost in my humanness. I felt a pull that I could not and would not resist toward love and peace in this life. I felt grateful that maybe that pull was coming from my loved ones on the other side.

Chapter 14

Seeing Life Through a New Lens

To my beautiful and wonderful Alie,

Hey Honey, I love you so much. I miss the human part of our relationship. Holding hands, even holding feet in bed, and your warm hugs. Our quiet times together, our walks, our fun times together, and our long talks. These are all human expressions and come from a deeper place of love beyond human and that is where we still and always will have our relationship. Dani shared a dream with me that she had where you said "yes" I am happy, you told her that she was dreaming, and you told her you are doing fine and that you are closer to Chris than you have ever been. It is so important for me to know that you are okay. You are amazing and deserve a great journey and I love and support you forever. I will continue my spiritual journey forward as well.

I love you forever and eternity.

Hey Chris,

My life was changed forever when you were born, and again when you died on the same day twenty-three years later. What a journey it has been. Thank you for all you have helped me to learn and continue to learn. It has not come without human sorrow and even suffering at some points. It was so painful for us left behind. My humanness still hurts and misses your humanness, but I am also blessed with some of the greatest revelations that have changed my human life so much, and let me embrace a spiritual relationship with you and now with Mom.

Love forever and eternity,
Dad

IN THE FIRST FEW months after Alie's death, I felt unbalanced and uncertain. Fortunately, I still had my business, where I could feel some level of routine and confidence in what I was doing. But outside of that, my life was upside down—from the day-to-day practical things of how to care for our pooches, how to work a washing machine, and how to pay our bills, to the much bigger issues of not having someone to talk to who understood me and loved me unconditionally, to trying to take on being a single parent to two beautiful daughters. I never realized how much Dani and Alex relied on their mom and how she was always there for them when I was working or out of town. We had such a great partnership in running our family that I must have taken it for granted until it wasn't there anymore.

I did my best to apply the lessons I had learned from grieving Christopher's death, but this time I did not have Alie by my side. I realized how much I'd relied on her strength. Being able to lean on each other made us stronger; on my own, there were new challenges to contend with. Chris's death had been sudden, and that let me play mind games where I could imagine he was just off to college and would be returning soon. I could find no such comfort in my imagination with Alie's death because we were with her every day and watched her deteriorate from a strong and fit tennis player to a frail body beaten up by cancer and its treatments. The oxygen machines, the lift chair and shower chair, and the seemingly endless bottles of medications that were in our home were constant reminders of her last weeks, and I made sure to remove them and get the house back to some normalcy.

My primary focus was to be available for my daughters, who had already lost their big brother at young, tender ages and now lost their mom at ages twenty-one and thirty-two. They would not have a mom for their weddings or to be a grandma to their children. I had never given much thought to these major life events because I always assumed Alie would be there to do what she does and make everything perfect. I soon realized I couldn't be Mom, but I was going to do my best to be the greatest dad I could be. Chris and Alie had moved on from their human experiences, and now Dani, Alex, and I needed to find the new normal in our lives without them by our sides.

We continued hosting Thanksgiving, which was a huge undertaking with almost twenty of our family members attending. Fortunately, Dani and Alex had inherited their mom's gifts for creating special occasions filled with love and warmth. We also continued our tradition of having a holiday party right around Chris's birthday, a week before Christmas, and had the whole family come by to share the cheer and celebrate Chris and Alex's birthdays as well.

I felt so fortunate that both of our daughters had grown up to be so wise in knowing that family always comes first. Dani and Alex would often express their concern for me, checking in to make sure I was doing okay moving through these tough early times. Alie had prepared them well, and I can feel her legacy in the warmth, love, and thoughtfulness in all they do for me and our family.

Before she became ill, Alie and I had enjoyed many happy times imagining the future we would share once I sold my business. Many of our friends lived in country clubs with beautiful tennis courts and golf courses, and we talked about buying a home in one of them, where we could maintain an active social life and keep up with the sports we both enjoyed. Alie's death changed all that. I now had to be open to an entirely new chapter in my life that I had never planned for. This world of uncertainty was scary at times, but I always felt within my heart that I would be okay. I knew that by staying open, I would be led in the right direction. I felt drawn to spiritual people, retreats, and communities and sensed that these things would be a big part of my future. I was doing my best to accept that life does what it does and was unfolding perfectly. While I and everyone are all part of that perfect design, it is difficult, and maybe impossible as humans, to see a large enough context to understand this perfection completely.

When I journaled with Alie, I would sometimes ask her if she now saw or understood this larger context of life unfolding perfectly from her new formless perspective. I found that I was asking this question because I still wasn't able to fully embrace this perfection when it included the deaths of Alie and Chris at such young ages and the many other horrific things that happen around the world. Why would a loving God, Universe, or Source allow these things to happen if all was perfect?

In my voracious reading and searching for answers, I found that Michael Singer's work provided me with context that gave me some level of peace. He would discuss how the universe has been evolving perfectly for over thirteen billion years and has billions of galaxies that each have billions of suns with their own solar systems. This evolution has gone on perfectly for all this time and has not needed our opinions, judgments, or beliefs, and so why would it need them now? Is our universe so vast that our human mind cannot comprehend or see a big enough picture of it to see its perfection? After all, we are living on only one small speck of this grand and expanding universe on our tiny and beautiful planet Earth.

I realized that while we have been given the gift to consciously observe, recognize, and even understand the grandeur and magnificence of the Universe from scientific discoveries and the use of their amazing telescopes, we struggle to truly realize its perfection. However, we can innately *feel* its perfection when we quiet our minds and recognize that we are an extension or expression of this vast universal energy that has precisely and flawlessly evolved over these billions of years. Rather than feeling insignificant in the immensity of that of which we are a part, we can accept its perfection and know it as the reality that is flowing through us, gives us life, and is our essence.

Recognizing Samskaras

My understanding of why it seems so difficult to see the perfection of life became clearer when Singer introduced me to the Sanskrit term *samskara,* which I had never heard before. The most basic meaning of a samskara is that it is a blockage caused by unreconciled emotions that continues to affect us throughout our life. An example would be if you were bit by a dog as a child, you might continue to carry the fear of dogs into your adult life if that emotion is not addressed and released.

Michael Singer went on to say that our life experiences are based on the events that come in through our senses, of which our consciousness then becomes aware. A beautiful aspect of human life is that all our experiences are truly gifts for us to learn from, whether they be pleasurable or painful. The perfection of life is always occurring and is in the present moment; the only problem is that we sometimes don't like or agree with how life is unfolding. Certain events may make us feel sad or mad or fearful, and so we do not let the experience flow through us. Instead, we block the internal experience, bury or deny it, or blame someone or something else, and *this* causes us to feel that life is "imperfect."

That blockage or samskara is what we store in our mind, and it becomes a thing we cannot see past. So, while life itself is perfect, it's only in the times when we don't like or agree with what's happening that we say that there are problems, challenges, and even events that we don't approve or accept. We think that reality should change for us to feel better, or that resistance to it will make it better; yet reality doesn't change, and resistance doesn't help. Our true power is in our ability to choose how we will respond to reality as it unfolds.

Soon after Alie passed away, I had a life-changing and very scary experience that caused me to become acutely aware of whether I was going to let life flow and respond appropriately or resist. My daughters knew that I never went to doctors, and for many years they were fine with that. But after Alie died so suddenly, they became adamant that I should go for a complete physical to be sure I was healthy. At the time, I didn't even have a family doctor, but I found a local primary care physician through one of the doctors who treated Alie. He did a complete physical, and all seemed good except for the fact that my PSA level was high.

I initially responded by ignoring the results, rationalizing that all would be fine. But within a few months, I noticed some symptoms that were causing me discomfort. I finally made an appointment with a urologist on the strong suggestion of my primary care doctor. By that time, my PSA level had gone through the roof. I was immediately sent for a biopsy and diagnosed with Stage IV prostate cancer that had metastasized into my bone. My initial reaction was shock, fear, and concern for my daughters. Dani and Alex had lost their mom just a year or so before, and now they had to deal with their dad having a possibly life-threatening disease.

I knew this was the time to apply all the tools I'd been working with for years. I needed to accept the reality of how my life was unfolding, embrace it as a lesson, surrender it to a higher power, and then take action steps that made sense in treating the cancer. I found an excellent oncologist, as well as alternative approaches that resonated with me. Most importantly, because I chose acceptance instead of resistance, I kept a healthy attitude and did not identify with the disease in any way. I found that by mentally moving away from the label of cancer and all its associated fearful narratives, I could accept that I had some cells in chaos that needed to be rebalanced. This mindset gave me confidence that there was a pathway to healing while I did all the necessary physical, mental, emotional, and spiritual work to live a healthy lifestyle.

My commitment to staying in the observer position and not reacting to the fear and worry that were so prominent was the first huge step. I accepted the situation and put a plan in place to handle it. This gave me the total responsibility and power to experience life on my terms. By taking the observer position, the experience of this diagnosis became an important opportunity for me to become aware of my buried samskaras—the biggest one by far being the fear of death. By creating a space between *who I am* and the samskara, I could see beyond it, honor my fears and worries, and let them go.

This major life experience and lesson taught me so much. I now find that if a person, place, thing, or event causes me to feel anxious, angry, worried, fearful, or anything other than compassionate, calm, and at peace, I know I am experiencing a samskara. With this awareness, I know that I need to let go, allow life to flow through me, and choose how to respond from a loving place.

Forgiveness Is a Bridge

One of the great "channeled" books of our time, *The Way of Mastery*, outlines the steps of spiritual growth. Growth is initially energized by the *desire* to awaken, followed by an *intention* to move past our fears. The next big leap is *allowing* for life to unfold through us without resistance, and finally a *surrender* to the source of all life. These tools of desire, intention, allowing, and surrender work because they are all based in love. Following these steps can bring us to a state of mastery in which life unfolds effortlessly for the highest good of all.

I practiced allowing these qualities to guide me and found that they had the effect of moving me out of my self-centered ego with its wants, needs, and disappointments and into a state in which life simply unfolds. I didn't engage as much with my fears and worries, or overthink decisions, stress out over pursuing goals, or try to understand the meaning of human events. Instead, I tried to remember that by staying in the Now, I was part of the perfection of each moment, and that my job in this lifetime was to be a student and greet each experience with an open mind of curiosity and gratitude.

In addition to these four critical traits of desire, intention, allowing, and surrender, I have also found that forgiveness is a powerful tool that helps me get much closer to my truth. Many spiritual masters have discussed forgiveness at great length, explaining how it is a bridge that gets us from reacting from the outside-in to responding from the inside-out. The recent cancer diagnosis required every bit of my strength to apply what I had been learning about these tools, especially forgiveness.

I recognized that it was fear that delayed me from acknowledging that I had a physical condition that needed attention. I was given a clear red flag by the PSA results but reacted to it from the outside in by fearing it, then refusing to acknowledge the fear, and then burying it within me as a samskara. I had to move to an inside-out attitude and take responsibility, which became my desire and intention. Next, I had to accept the reality of how life was unfolding through me, surrender it to a higher power, and take conscious action. Forgiving myself for reacting with fear and ignoring reality then helped me expand my context and see this challenge as a gift to help me grow.

The best definition of forgiveness I have ever come across is from *The Way of Mastery*: "Forgiveness is forgiveness of one's self for insisting on replacing reality with our own version of it." This definition very succinctly and directly places the choice for forgiveness in our total control and tells us that the only one we need to forgive is ourselves because we chose incorrectly. We made a mistake by choosing to give some person, place, thing, circumstance, or experience a meaning that was not based in reality. Our decision was based in our programming, but now we can choose to see it differently, always returning to the question, "What would love do now?"

When I looked back on the early days after Christopher's death, I realized that so much of my mental energy was going into trying to replace reality with my version of it. This created resistance and suffering. In the years since, I have come to accept reality on a deep level, paving the way for true forgiveness and gratitude to occur. I am committed to the practices of observing, being aware of when my samskaras get triggered, and making responsible choices that will provide more peace in my life. The feeling of peace within has always been the best barometer I know that confirms I am coming from my higher self and not from ego.

Allowing Life's Meaning

As the years went on after Chris's passing, and now that Alie, too, had died, I had become more and more introspective. My context for viewing life became larger, and I was more compassionate and forgiving. I very much liked this emerging self. It gave me a feeling of peace and calm. I was more comfortable accepting and embracing the mystery instead of trying to know all the answers. I continued my pursuit of spiritual conversations with a growing group of people in my life who shared my commitment to helping each other awaken. I placed even less importance on reacting to my emotions and more on the lessons that were inherent in them.

Many spiritual masters have spoken about a thin veil that makes us feel that we are separate from our source. This veil feels real when we look at our separate bodies and our separate opinions and beliefs and all our justifications and rationalizations, our need to be right and our need to win. This illusion of separation is what gives rise to the world of constant change, complexity, comparison, and chaos. This is the insanity our society has created, which can seem so real when we look at the world from an outside-in lens. Yet when we switch to an inside-out lens, the fog clears and we can feel our connection to the Source of all life.

I often imagine what it would be like if I could totally suspend my incessant mind chatter—the running commentary in my head primarily made up of opinions, beliefs, and judgments triggered by outside stimuli coming in through my senses. During moments of meditation, I would often practice finding a short period where this noisy loop of thinking would cool down and get as close to silence as possible. This would always make me feel much closer to my essence, which was peaceful—indeed, to recognizing my connection to everyone and everything and feeling a sense of oneness with life.

I remembered a day long ago, while I was journaling with Chris, when I was angry and questioning life. In that moment I realized that questioning life's plan made no sense, as I didn't have the ability to understand something so vast. Chris was well on his journey, and the better question I needed to ask was, *What does the experience of Chris's death mean to my life and my growth?* This realization moved me from asking why and the mental chatter of thoughts about what could have been and all that I'd lost to a much larger perspective. When put in the context of my growth and my journey forward, it felt like a release.

By observing myself during these times of communication with Chris, I also began to view all of life in a different way. Instead of constantly trying to find the Meaning of Life, I was allowing life to have meaning *through me*. When the mental noise quieted to a place of stillness, I could accept that Chris leaving his humanness at twenty-three years old was part of life's plan. I may not agree or understand why, but I could accept it. I could also accept that it is Chris's journey and my journey on our path of growth. This more aligned mindset with life made me realize that growth can come more and more from conscious acceptance and surrender rather than from the suffering of resistance.

A New Beginning

For years before Alie passed, we'd spent a lot of time talking about me winding down and selling my business. The firm had been a huge part of both of our lives, and Alie was known as the "First Lady," enjoying all she did to make our employees feel so welcomed and appreciated. Our staff were also my biggest source of enjoyment and first priority. I thoroughly enjoyed interacting with all of them, especially the mentoring work I was doing with both new and experienced advisors. My colleagues had been there for me through thick and thin, providing me with incredible support when I needed it most, and I felt immensely privileged to have enjoyed such a wonderful career.

The dream had always been that Christopher would be the third generation to continue the success of the business, which had been built over more than fifty years. Instead, I needed to develop a successor team that had experience and would carry on the family culture. This process took a few years, but eventually I put a team in place that would continue to grow the firm while allowing me to enjoy watching from afar. I was totally prepared to move on, although I did not have a plan for how that would occur. I always felt that I would be guided in some way. I knew I was not the type to watch old *Seinfeld* reruns all day, and I knew that my life would be centered around my spiritual practice.

Finally, two years after Alie died, I officially sold my company. Just like that, I was no longer a CEO. Life had changed completely, both personally and now professionally. I found that having no outside identity moved me away from some of the superficial conversations of "what I do" to more meaningful conversations about who I really am. I felt gratitude for the great run I had in business and for the amazing life I spent with Alie. It was now time to move on into a totally new chapter where I would have time to focus on this mysterious thing called my life. I had no plan for this but am so grateful that writing this book has been a wonderful result of life guiding me so far. My new purpose was becoming clearer every day.

Chapter 15

Resistance or Flow

Hey Chris,

Our experience has taught me that life is eternal; therefore, there is no such thing as death. My attachment to the physical body makes it seem like life can end, but this is an illusion. I can remember so many times when I would come to your bedroom and you were sleeping. I would look at you and feel the same love even though you were sound asleep and not conscious I was there. Whether your humanness is conscious or not, our love and relationship is ongoing. You are helping me realize how much deeper love goes and is so far beyond this human dimension. Thank you for this understanding.

Love forever and eternity,
Dad

WHEN I STARTED LOOKING back over the thousands of journal entries I had made since Christopher's death, I felt so fortunate to relive the tiny steps I was taking. My journaling showed me the slow but sure process of continued learning I was going through, even at times when the grief and sadness seemed unbearable. The process of growth and ultimately transformation can make you feel like you aren't making any progress much of the time. But it's like watching a tree grow: If you stand there staring at it, you'll feel like nothing's happening, but if you come back over months and years, it is a marvel to see its growth. Although I was lost and uncertain at first, my journals are a record of increasing trust in the path that was unfolding before me.

It is now two decades after Christopher's death. I have learned that the way I experience this human life is determined by how much I resist it or how much I allow it to flow. In every moment, I can choose to have an attitude of either willingness or resistance. Willingness means being open to the flow of life and recognizing that every experience I have is exactly what I need to awaken. It is living in the present moment, which aligns me with my purpose and the purpose of the universe. Resistance, which takes the form of opinions, judgments, likes, and dislikes, closes my mind and shrinks my perspective. I can find myself living in a very small and narrow-minded world when I'm stuck in the thoughts in my head.

Allowing life to flow isn't as hard as it sounds. After all, most of us *already* allow life to flow through us most of the time without even realizing it. We have so many experiences on a day-to-day and even minute-to-minute basis, like driving or walking along and seeing countless trees and land and buildings and people and scenery. We allow most of this sensory input to simply flow through us, and that is one of the beautiful aspects of human life. Our minds are certainly *aware* of the landscape passing by, but there is nothing within us that grabs on and holds it. Instead, we enjoy it and let it go, and this is happening most of the time.

On the other hand, we all have experiences where we *block* this flow. For example, many of us have had a near miss while driving when a deer runs out in front of the car, forcing us to brake or swerve. Even though the danger may pass in a matter of seconds, we often hold onto the fear, telling ourselves stories about all the terrible things that could have happened.

We replay the experience over and over in our minds, mixing it with thinking and resistance, not allowing our bodies to recover from the original shock. We even continue the fearful thoughts and scenarios and share them with others. When we are in a state of awareness, however, we can observe the feeling of fear, allow it to flow through us, and choose to feel gratitude that we and the deer are unhurt. We can then return to the present moment, going back to our enjoyment of the drive and the scenery without getting stuck.

This is true for every life experience, up to and including tragedy and loss. We can choose to resist and be angry at life for the death of a loved one; we can remain trapped in stories of what could have been and the many ways the loss continues to cause us misery. Or we can allow the pain to move through us, feel it without denying it, and surrender it to a power greater than ourselves.

This path of allowing life to flow leads to an attitude of openness and curiosity, as opposed to suppressing the pain and turning it into blockages. This is why I have found it so important to continually remind myself to stay in the observer position and to be mindful and purposeful in my choices of how I respond to life.

The Eight-Step Grief to Gratitude Journey

One of the great musicians, songwriters, and artists of our time, Bruce Springsteen, said when pondering the death of his mom and other loved ones, "Death leaves a final gift to those that are still living; it gives us an expanded view of life."

When I look back over all the lessons I've learned since Christopher's death, eight stand out as being the most critical and life-changing. Each of these insights shifted my mindset in profound ways, opening me up to new possibilities.

While I wish that Chris and Alie were still here, and I miss them very much, I am eternally grateful for these experiences, as they have become an important part of my growth and awakening. These new paradigms for viewing death provided a larger context that relieved some of my suffering and enabled my life to move forward on a peaceful path. I offer them here as guidelines for anyone who may be going through grief, loss, or other life challenges, along with journaling prompts that helped me express my feelings.

Acknowledge grief and accept that life is here to teach us and not torture us.

Key Concepts: Start by accepting that grief is a natural human response. Sadness, anger, and confusion hurt and feel real, but they are not who we are. Although we may not *like* everything that happens in our lives, we can develop wisdom by recognizing that every experience is a lesson for our spiritual awakening. By adopting a student mindset, we can ease our resistance to reality as it unfolds and open ourselves to learning and living a more peaceful life.

Journaling Prompt: Write down what you are feeling. Let your feelings flow freely onto the page without thinking or censorship. Feel the pain and do not fear it, as even this emanates from love and occurs for our growth.

Look at death from "their" side.

Key Concepts: When a loved one dies, it is natural and necessary to grieve and focus on our own pain and sorrow, as well as any anger, guilt, and regret we may feel. In the midst of these intense emotions, remembering to look at this experience from our loved one's perspective will help ease our suffering. When we step outside the point of view that labels death as "the end" or as a "personal" loss, we can see a bigger context in which their life was perfectly designed to last exactly as long as it did. Even though we may not like this design or agree with it, we have the choice to support their journey and release ourselves from the limited personal perspective, and this creates space for acceptance

Journaling Prompt: Write to your loved one about how you support their ongoing journey and about what you think they would want for you in this moment.

Focus on what can be instead of what could have been.

Key Concepts: After a loved one dies, our minds can easily spin stories of all the things that could or should have happened if they had lived. This distracts us from the important fact that we are still in a relationship with our loved one. By focusing on what *can still be* and finding new ways to feel close to our loved one, we put that ongoing relationship front and center. We then recognize the enormous potential for continued growth in the present instead of clinging to an imaginary future that will never be.

Journaling Prompt: Write about your vision for moving forward and how this experience might be guiding you to grow. Reflect on what lessons, insights, or strengths are emerging and how your loss makes you more aware of your ongoing spiritual relationship with your loved one.

Seek awareness, not sympathy; journaling as therapy.

Key Concepts: Finding someone to talk to who will listen rather than giving us pity and sympathy is a tremendous asset. Although it can be tempting to stay in a space of self-pity, especially when speaking with someone, journaling is a tremendous outlet for expressing our innermost feelings. Allowing ourselves to follow our stream of consciousness is much more likely to bring us closer to our truth. It's critical to remind ourselves that we owe it to our loved ones to find a higher meaning for this traumatic and life-changing experience than simply feeling sorry for ourselves and to set a strong intention to find this meaning.

Journaling Prompt: Commit to journaling as a new language and expression that gets you closer to meaning and truth. Write about what you are holding on to that no longer serves you and how your life might shift if you released these feelings.

Separate emotions from identity.

Key Concepts: Grief, sadness, and other emotions do not define you but need to be observed and allowed to flow. Fully feeling the emotions allows their energy to burn itself out. We need to practice patience and compassion for ourselves during this time, because these feelings hurt. We also need to do our best to remain in the observer position and not engage the emotions with thought or identify them as who we are, which is what turns them into an imaginary story with no reality and causes suffering.

Journaling Prompt: Write about your emotions in the third person and reflect on your true self, which is your passions and the qualities of your life that bring you joy and fulfillment.

Recognize that love is a bond at a spiritual level.

Key Concepts: Love is eternal and is not limited to our time together in this human experience. It is a bond that cannot be broken by death and which does not require a physical body. You can feel this bond by journaling with your loved one, having ongoing conversations with them, meditating, walking in nature, spending quiet time in stillness, and remembering that the human form is just a temporary container and our spiritual reality is eternal.

Journaling Prompt: Write about the love you still share with your loved one and how this feeling continues to grow and impact your life today. How does acknowledging this love, beyond the physical, shape and guide your life?

Embrace the love within.

Key Concepts: Love isn't something we get from other people; it's a feeling we naturally have within ourselves. Sharing our love is what expands the feeling and makes it stronger. When a loved one dies, the love we felt for them doesn't disappear. It continues uninterrupted as long as we remain connected to it.

Journaling Prompt: Write about the love you feel for those who have passed on and for those who are still in your life. How does expressing this compassion and love for others feel as you move forward in your healing process?

Practice gratitude, as it is the great healer.

Key Concepts: Although the pain of grief can feel unbearable, accepting the perfection of life and knowing that its challenges are designed for our growth will ultimately lead to gratitude for the experience. This gratitude certainly has nothing to do with the person's death but everything to do with the lessons we learn from the experience that lead to a more fulfilling and awakened life. Gratitude is the ultimate step in the alchemy that transforms suffering back into love.

Journaling Prompt: Write about three things you are grateful for each day. They can be small or large, but let them center around your growth, the love you feel, and how you are living in this new normal with a grateful heart.

These eight insights, combined with daily journaling, empowered me and helped me handle the unimaginable experience of my son's death and later Alie's death. I hope they will serve as useful guidelines for you or anyone else who is seeking answers in the wake of a serious loss.

A Path with Purpose

There is a purpose for everything in life—life could not be otherwise. There is no chaos, no mistakes, or accidents; it's just that we are unable to see a big enough picture to understand life's perfection, and so we often respond with fear in the face of this uncertainty. The only sane way to live is to appreciate the flow of life, accept it, and respond to it from our highest self, knowing that we are a part of this grand universe and its continued perfect unfolding.

This unfolding has been going on for fourteen billion years without our opinions and judgments and certainly does not need our agreement or approval now. Instead, we need to humbly and gratefully accept that we have been granted the gift of a human life on this beautiful planet Earth.

Scientists estimate that the probability of being born a human is about one in four hundred trillion. The Buddha said, "Rare is it to be born a human; rarer still is it to have heard of enlightenment; and most rare is it to pursue enlightenment." In other words, we are blessed to have a human life. We need to remember how lucky we are and appreciate each and every experience during this short time, knowing that we are all given exactly what we need to handle the challenges and continue to grow.

We are never alone in this journey. Spiritual masters who have gone before us have pointed the way and spoken about following our inner guidance, which is always pulling us with gentle love. There are also many more than we realize on this path, and we should feel gratitude for living during this time.

Keeping ourselves in a mindset of awe for the perfection of this universe, combined with this deep gratitude for the blessing of our human life, creates an atmosphere where we can grow from sadness, anger, and grief to compassion, love, and awakening.

As much as Chris and Alie's deaths hurt so badly, these experiences had the potential to open the window to my growth. Those whom we love so deeply who have gone to the other side have given us a gift that can lead us to becoming aware of our spiritual nature. There can be no greater gift, and I thank my son Christopher and my wife Alie for this blessing every day.

And I thank you, dear reader, for allowing me to share. My only purpose is to help relieve some of the unimaginable suffering felt by so many when a close loved one dies. I truly hope that I have expressed my experiences, and the insights learned from them, in a way that can lead to healing for you, just as they continue to do for me.

Love forever and eternity.

Acknowledgments

UNBEKNOWN TO ME, THIS book began its birth on the day my son died. The daily journaling from that darkest day of my life and for twenty years afterward took me from the deepest depths of sorrow to eventually opening the path to awakening. I did not walk this path alone, and there are so many to whom I owe a profound debt of gratitude.

To my beloved son, Chris, and to my wife, Alie, whose love was unconditional—your departures shattered my heart, yet your continued presence has brought me light, purpose, and the profound reminder that love transcends form.

To my daughters, Dani and Alex—who, through even their unimaginable heartache, were always there to support me, and we continue to learn and grow together. And to my dad and my sister Patty, who allowed me to express my raw emotions and spiritual revelations each step along the way. To my fiancée, Jeanne—thank you for listening to each new iteration of every paragraph with enthusiasm, patience, and encouragement.

To the spiritual teachers who shaped my understanding of life's deeper truths—beginning with the Concept-Therapy Institute, Dr. Thurman Fleet, and Char and Emily Mattox. To my spiritual coach, Joe Tedesco, whose guidance and presence were invaluable. And to the contemporary masters whose teachings became spiritual companions on this journey: Eckhart Tolle, David Hawkins, Michael Singer, Deepak Chopra, and *A Course in Miracles*.

To Jack Canfield—thank you for your generous endorsement, for seeing the soul of this work, and for encouraging me to share it with the world. Your words offered affirmation at a time when they were most needed.

To my editor, Hilary Smith—thank you for your dedication, clarity, and collaboration throughout the better part of a year, helping me shape my raw writing into a manuscript ready for the world. To the early readers of the manuscript and the entire professional support team—thank you for your patience, insight, and commitment to honoring the message of this work.

And finally, all glory goes to God in the Highest—the Source and Mystery of Life—for which I have the deepest humility and gratitude. Thank You for allowing this life to be lived on the Inner Pathway.

With love and reverence,

Steve Ferrara

Journal Notes

STEVEN FERRARA has been a lifelong student seeking the inner pathway to peace and awakening while helping others on their journeys.

For more than two decades, he taught a course in universal and spiritual principles for the Concept-Therapy Institute as part of a nationally recognized teaching team with his father and sister. Influenced by *A Course in Miracles* and the works of Eckhart Tolle, David Hawkins, and Michael Singer, Steven has developed a deep understanding of the healing potential of forgiveness and gratitude. His dedication to meditation, which started when he took a transcendental meditation class as a teenager, has helped him embrace the power in the present moment and to continue to know that inner peace.

As a business leader, Steven built a small family insurance business into a large financial services company, serving as CEO for twenty-five years before selling the company in 2020 to focus entirely on his spiritual journey. He was a sought-after speaker at national conferences, where he led countless workshops on business and life coaching.

The tragic loss of his twenty-three-year-old son, Christopher, and later the death of his beloved wife, Alie, profoundly challenged Steven's spiritual understanding. This led him to explore grief and seek a new perspective on death and life, embarking on a journey toward the transformative healing power of gratitude and a pathway to inner peace.

Steven is devoted to his family with two daughters, Dani and Alex, their growing families, and his fiancée, Jeanne. He has always made family and his commitment to personal growth and awakening his utmost priority. He lives in Delray Beach, Florida, and enjoys staying active, riding motorcycles, and engaging in deep, meaningful conversations.

LEARN MORE AT STEVENFERRARA.COM

Twenty percent of all author proceeds from book sales will go to the Christopher Foundation to support consciousness research.